AYAHUASCA
A NEAR-DEATH TRANSFORMATION

Discovery Publisher

Author: Adriano Lucca
Translation (UK English— 1st-pass): Samuel Geddes-Coyle
Translation (US English): Anderson Warren
Editing: Anderson Warren & Adriano Lucca

616 Corporate Way
Valley Cottage, New York, 10989
www.discoverypublisher.com
edition@discoverypublisher.com
facebook.com/discoverypublisher
twitter.com/discoverypb

New York • Paris • Dublin • Tokyo • Hong Kong

TABLE OF CONTENTS

AYAHUASCA
A NEAR-DEATH TRANSFORMATION

An old Cherokee chief once told his grandson, "There is a war that rages inside us all. It is a war between two wolves. One represents all that is bad; he is anger, envy, guilt, sadness and ego. The other represents all that is good; he is joy, love, hope, truth and faith."

The grandson asked, "Grandpa, which wolf wins?"

The chief replied, "The one you feed."

To my family, for their unconditional
support during my journeys.

To Aesha, Asil, Hernan, Ian, Rory, Scott and Yogesh,
for their beautiful friendship and invaluable advice.

Dear Reader,

Before diving headlong into some of the adventures recounted in this book, make sure you are in excellent health, both in body and mind. Prior to participating in any shamanic activity, whether it involves ayahuasca, kambó, sananga, rapé or other shamanic practices, make sure the shamans and the organizers are aware of any medical conditions you may have.

Although the author has made every attempt to make the reader fully aware of the risks that can be encountered when participating in the activities and ceremonies described in these pages, neither the author nor the publisher takes any responsibility for any incident, accident or other adverse consequence which may result from the practice of ayahuasca and/or shamanism.

———

To protect the privacy of certain individuals, their names have been changed.

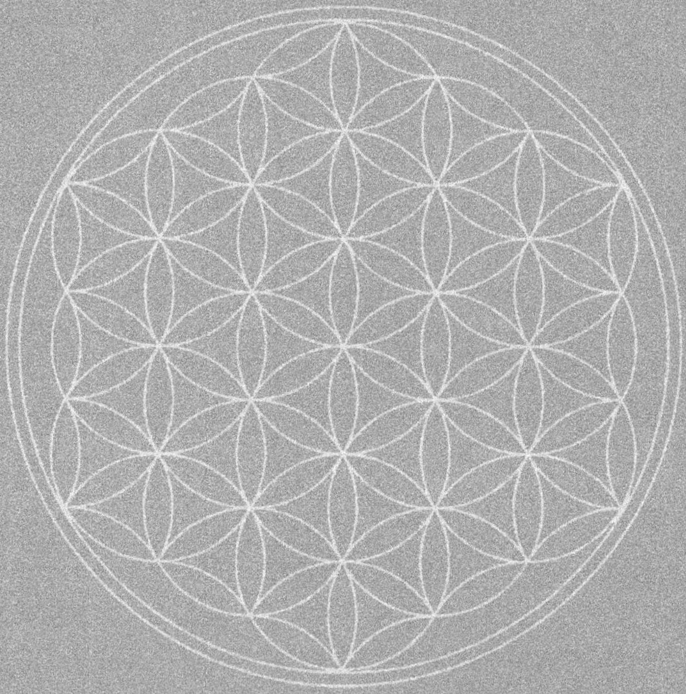

A Timely Coincidence

Beauty is the harmony of chance and kindness.
— Simone Weil

September 27, 2016, Dharamshala, India

I sat down next to Yogesh and closed the taxi door. Aesha was in the front, on the driver's side.

"What are you going to do next?" I asked Yogesh.

"Aesha and I are planning to go to the Amazon to take part in ayahuasca ceremonies," replied Yogesh.

"The Amazon... Ayahuasca!," I repeated involuntarily, very surprised.

My initial reaction was that this young couple did not fit my preconceived idea of ayahuasca consumers. Even though my knowledge of shamanism was very limited at that time, I had heard of this famous decoction, the fearsome "vine of the dead" also known as "the plant which opens the door to the spirit world".

We had just finished a silent yoga retreat in a Himalayan refuge two hours from Dharamshala, a small town in northern India. Apart from our first names and exchanging smiles during communal meals and the endless yoga and meditation sessions, we did not know much about each other. I am not very good at remembering names, I forget them easily. It is only once I have become close to someone that I can remember their name. However, I rarely forget a face, even if I have only seen it briefly. The same goes for first impressions. Yogesh and Aesha made a very good impression on me; they seemed a lovely couple.

I was already well into my gap year, and my time in India was coming to an end. With my tourist visa about to expire, I was keen to decide on my next destination. What my two friends had just told me opened my eyes to new possibilities. Straightening in my seat and looking at Yogesh and Aesha in turn, I said:

"Your plan is really interesting. In fact, I've been thinking about trying ayahuasca for some time, but I've never had the opportunity or it's never the *right* time. Your plans seem… Hmm… Tell me…"

I paused. I was worried that I was going to receive a negative answer to my burning question, but I quickly continued:

"Can I join you?"

Surprised by my sudden excitement for their plans, but having promptly received agreement from Aesha, who gave a timid smile and a small nod, Yogesh threw his hands up in the air and, laughing, said:

"Sure, why not!"

During the rest of the journey to McLeod Ganj, a suburb of Dharamshala known as "the Little Lhasa" because of its large population of Tibetans and the fact that the Dalai Lama has his main residence there, I noted down as many details as possible about the shamanic festival. Yogesh promised to let me have the personal email address of the organizer once he had access to the Internet.

In the evening, my two friends and I, along with other members of our group, dined at a charming Italian restaurant in Dharamkot, a little hill above McLeod Ganj. During the meal, we exchanged our thoughts on the yoga and meditation course that we had just finished and our discussions naturally turned to spiritual matters. It was then that Jeff, an American who had also taken part in the course, stopped suddenly mid-sentence, straightened in his chair, stared at me and, in an almost solemn voice, asked:

"Adriano, have you ever tried ayahuasca?"

This took me by surprise. We had been talking about yoga, Vedanta and other related subjects on spirituality in India. There were no indications that this topic was going to be brought up.

"No Jeff, but it's very strange that you should mention ayahuasca… Well, a very interesting coincidence at least. Yogesh, Aesha and I were just talking about it in the taxi on the way back," I replied, turning to look at Yogesh.

"You must know that there are no coincidences when it comes to ayahuasca!" Jeff exclaimed turning to Yogesh, who, with a knowing smile, nodded in agreement.

Once the meal was finished, I said my goodbyes to the group and went to speak to Yogesh and Aesha.

"Don't forget to send me the email address of the festival organizer, okay?" I said.

Aesha assured me she would do so that same night and I promised I would see them a few weeks later on the frontier of the Amazon.

During the weeks that followed, I questioned myself numerous times whether I was doing the right thing. However, when I was just about to renounce the idea of attending ayahuasca ceremonies, I would come across a similar coincidence as while in India. The more it happened, the more I felt that I should not ignore them, that I should 'follow the signs'.

I did not know then that the spirits of the forest and that of ayahuasca were going to take me on the most intense, most terrifying, and yet, the most transformational experience of my life.

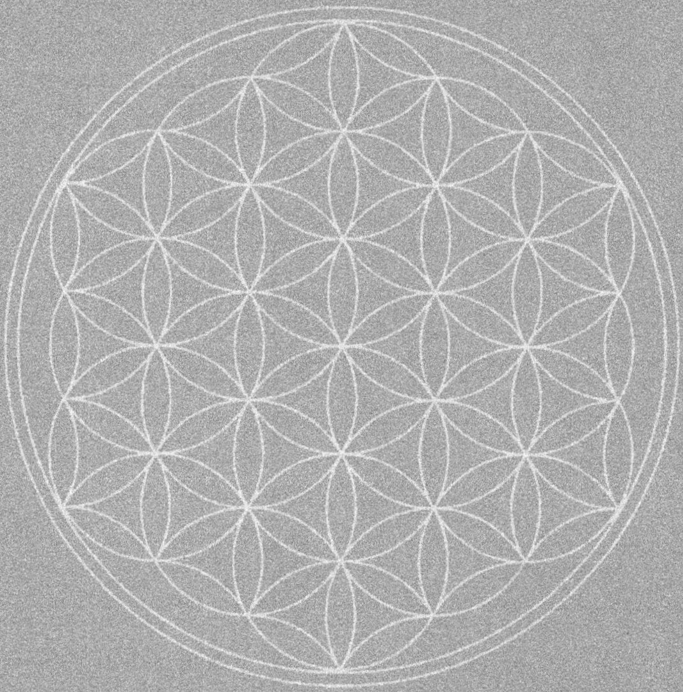

Spirituality and Ayahuasca

Spirituality is the least of our worries
before it becomes our biggest regret.
— André Frossard

After leaving India, I carried out some research into shamanism and ayahuasca. One significant thing I learned was that shamanism is neither a religion nor a philosophy, but an ancient practice which involves a first-hand experience with the universal consciousness. Through it, we renew our awareness that we are an integral part of the universe. To a large extent, the vast majority of people, particularly those living in industrialized and economically developed countries, lost this ability a long time ago.

In the lingua franca of Quechua, a Native American language spoken in Peru and Bolivia, 'ayahuasca' (pronounced 'ay-ee-u-aska' with a very soft 'ee') means 'vine of the soul' or 'vine of the dead'. However, the term 'ayahuasca' has come to mean both the caapi[1] plant, a species of tropical vine found in the Amazon, and an aqueous preparation, of which it is the sole or main ingredient. Today, when we talk about ayahuasca, we generally mean the

---

1. Banisteriopis caapi: this vine is found in the tropical regions of Peru, Bolivia, Brazil, Venezuela and Panama and on the pacific coastline of Colombia and Ecuador.

concoction consumed during shamanic ceremonies of the same name. The most widely known of these concoctions is a normally highly concentrated preparation obtained via a one- or two-step slow-cooking process taking six to eight hours in total and starting with a mixture of pre-washed and crushed lengths of caapi vine, chacruna[1] leaves and water.

According to specialized works on shamanism, the use of ayahuasca predates the modern era by several thousands of years. However, nobody has been able to confirm this fact with certainty. All that we can say is that this practice was already widespread amongst many indigenous tribes of the Amazon basin by the time Western anthropologists discovered it in the middle of the 19th century[2].

In the Amazon, shamanism and ayahuasca are currently the chosen keepers of spiritual and therapeutic practices. From a medical standpoint, there are numerous reports that certain serious physical and mental illnesses, which have often been deemed incurable, have been cured through ayahuasca ceremonies. More generally, it is noted that one's vital forces are rejuvenated and the person is freed from emotional blockages. On a spiritual level, biographical accounts often relate an awakening of one's intuition, spiritual abilities and the discovery of the hidden meaning of one's inner-

---

1. Psychotria viridis: a perennial plant of the Rubiaceae family.

2. The first reports of the psychoactive effects of the Banisteriopis caapi plant in Western scientific publications date back to 1851, from Peru. By the middle of the 1850s, numerous reports about its uses had been published in the Occident. In 1922—1923, a film showing an ayahuasca ceremony was screened at the annual conference for the American Pharmaceutical Association. By the end of the 20th century, ayahuasca shamanic ceremonies had become so popular that they gave rise to 'ayahuasca tourism'.

most self. As a matter of fact, once blockages have been removed, one becomes again in harmony with the higher self—the soul—as well as the universe.

The ayahuasca preparation contains DMT[1], a powerful psychotropic substance which, when consumed, can profoundly alter one's consciousness. Scientists have been fascinated by DMT for many years. Through their research, they have discovered that this molecule is present everywhere in nature; in plants, in animals, and even in the human body. In humans, DMT is naturally produced by the pineal gland, a tiny pine cone-shaped organ located between the two hemispheres of the brain. The precise function of this gland is not yet fully understood. Scientists have observed that it has an impact on sleep cycles, regulates sexual development, and is extremely sensitive to waves. Yet, Descartes had already defined it as 'the seat of the soul' and many cultures throughout history have called this gland the 'third eye'. According to Hindu, Tibetan, Egyptian and many other beliefs, it facilitates a connection with the afterlife, with the world of the spirits and the dead. In his writings, the famous Aldous Huxley states that DMT is 'the key which opens the door to the spirit world'. Certain studies carried out today go so far as to connect the experience of imminent death to the production of DMT by the pineal gland.

Huxley likened the brain to a receptor. When functioning normally, it allows us to deal with and operate in what we would call 'the real world'[2]. Any alteration to this receptor risks changing the perception of reality and consciousness. The consumption of a psy-

1. Dimethyltryptamine (N,N-Dimethyltryptamine) or DMT.
2. Or 'Physical Matter Reality—PMR' as called by Robert Monroe.

choactive substance, or the advanced practice of disciplines such as meditation, expands the field of perception, allowing interaction with other realities, or dimensions. In shamanism, these interactions are called 'shamanic journeys'. Some people report journeys into the collective unconsciousness, others describe this process as a means of communicating with spirits or subtler worlds. These interactions, or journeys, are different for everyone; some have visual experiences, others feel energies around them and yet others obtain direct knowledge. Huxley also states that the power—or increase—of perception grows with experience.

Even though ayahuasca is mainly prepared with two plants, the caapi vine and chacruna leaves, only the chacruna leaves contain DMT. However, when the leaves are consumed on their own, they have a somewhat negligible psychedelic effect[1]. It is the caapi vine that allows the psychedelic substance to be fully absorbed by the brain.

Given that there are more than 80,000[2] plants in the Amazonian forest, of which about 10,000 are vines, and that caapi and chacruna have morphologically absolutely nothing in common, how did the indigenous Amazonian people discover this specific ayahuasca formula? Anthropologists and scientists believe that it was discovered by trial and error. Statistically, however, the probability of this is about one in several billion. When shamans are asked this question, their response is invariably the same: "The spirits of the forest guided our ancestors."

1. The absorption of DMT is impeded by the enzyme monoamine oxidase. The caapi vine contains monoamine oxidase inhibitors which are indispensable for the total absorption of the psychedelic substance by our brains.

2. Between 40,000 and 110,000 depending on the source.

✳ ✳ ✳

I am not a religious person per se. Despite the utmost respect for the life and works of those who established major philosophies and religions, I believe that nowadays, most of the organized religions only retain vestiges of their true meaning. The latter has been lost, or grossly distorted at best. That said, I am not an atheist either. Even though I do not have any proof, I believe that there is a divine intelligence which governs our universe, controlling each stage of our evolution. As can be seen by the innumerable works on this topic that fill our bookstores and libraries, I am not the only one to hold such convictions.

To assert that evolution happens exclusively via natural selection, as per the British naturalist Charles Darwin[1], or that it is simply the result of sheer coincidence seems absurd to me. The British astrophysicist, Fred Hoyle[2], declared that "The chance that higher life forms might have emerged in this way is comparable to the chance that a tornado sweeping through a junkyard might assemble a Boeing 747 from the materials therein"[3]. Anyone who has even briefly studied the human anatomy cannot help but be filled with awe by its countless mysteries. Two questions naturally arise: what is the intelligence responsible for this extraordinary creation? and,

---

1. Charles Darwin (1809—1882) and his famous work, *The Origin of Species* (or more completely, *On the Origin of Species by Means of Natural Selection, or the Preservation of Favoured Races in the Struggle for Life*).

2. Sir Fred Hoyle FRS was a British astronomer who formulated the theory of stellar nucleosynthesis.

3. According to Fred Hoyle's analysis, the probability of cellular life's arising from non-living matter (abiogenesis) was about one-in-$10^{40,000}$.

where did it come from? Even without delving into realms such as human thought and the human soul but confining my questioning strictly to the existence of the physical body, I find myself in a dilemma. Logically, if we are not the source of its creation, an intelligence superior to our own must therefore be. If we are the creator, as Darwin's theory indirectly asserts, shouldn't we possess total and complete control over our each muscle, organ and cell as well as our evolution? As we are incapable of this to a very large extent, is it not logical to come to the same conclusion that there is a superior intelligence behind our creation which steers our evolution? The answer seems obvious to me.

If we look at the human race throughout history, it is indisputable that it is constantly evolving. Sadhguru Jaggi Vasudev[1], a modern-day Indian sage, declared that one of the intrinsic characteristics of our species is its fundamental need to expand. "Man constantly wants to become more than he is," says the Indian guru. When Man expresses this essential need by frantically pursuing material possessions or by satisfying his physical senses, however, he quietly slips into a deep sleep whereby he forgets who he really is, which is above all a being endowed with a vast consciousness and capable of exploits that we today call 'myths'. Should he stubbornly hold on to his egotistical goals, the relentless machinery that orchestrates his evolution reminds him that it has other plans in store for him. If he continues to be obstinate, the light coming from his eyes loses its intensity, he become embittered, faces chronic depression, frequently falls ill and deteriorates until death frees him from his

1. Sadhguru Jaggi Vasudev (1957—) commonly known as Sadhguru, is a guru and Indian mystic, founder of the Isha Foundation, a not-for-profit yoga and spirituality organization.

agony and gives him the freedom that his soul clamors for with repressed sobs. This phenomenon is described far more captivatingly by Bernard Enginger[1] in *Sri Aurobindo or the Adventure of Consciousness* and his subsequent works.

True happiness seems to occur and last when it is nurtured by spiritual exploration. In other words, true happiness is only achievable through self-realization, that is, when we are in tune with who we really are, with our soul. Conversely, as mentioned above, suffering seems to be proportional to how far we find ourselves from this quest.

Looking at the countless creations and accomplishments that humans have left behind them over the centuries, it is clear that the path to creativity, realization, or self-realization, is not the same for everyone. It seems that there is no one formula, and everyone must find their own way. Some people only need a few years of yoga practice, meditation, recital of mantras, praying or regularly attending a temple to change their conscience for self-realization to occur. For many though, the task is more challenging, even laborious in some cases.

The late great Swami Vivekananda[2] believed that there are four different temperaments, and that each one has its own path to self-realization. According to the swami, someone who is eager to take action should follow the path of action[3], that is, Karma Yoga.

---

1. Bernard Enginger (1923—2007) also known as Satprem, a name given to him by his mentor, the Indian sage Sri Aurobindo (1872—1950).

2. Swami Vivekananda (1863 – 1902) was an Indian Hindu monk, a chief disciple of the 19th-century Indian mystic Ramakrishna.

3. Also called the path of abnegation in certain texts.

The person who is filled with unconditional love for everyone and everything should follow the path of devotion, Bhakti Yoga. An intellectual person should follow the path of knowledge, Jnana Yoga. And finally, a meditative or contemplative person should follow the path of conquering one's inner self—or inner energies, Raja Yoga[1]. Here, the word 'yoga' is used in the sense of union—the union between the individual consciousness and the universal consciousness—and not in the manner that we incorrectly use it today in the West, thereby limiting it exclusively to the physical exercises of this age-old practice.

Personally, not having obtained satisfying enough results from disciplines such as physical yoga exercises, meditation, martial arts, praying or selfless actions—which are more and more difficult to achieve in our materialistic societies, it seems that my path is that of knowledge. In fact, I have always been passionate about anything to do with history, nature and the evolution of humankind and his place in the universe. I have spent countless hours understanding and contemplating the connections between certain aspects of plants, animals, humans and the stars. However, even if it is a very valuable too, intellectual analysis has its limit in unravelling the innumerable mysteries of life. I have many questions but few answers. What is consciousness? What is life? What is their real purpose? Who created us? As a collective soul, have we unconsciously created this seemingly merciless world or have we been coerced into it by unscrupulous demons? Why does the spiritual path often only reveal itself in times of suffering? Why is surrendering to pleasures so natural when the spiritual path is often lined with thorns? Why

---

1. Also known as Kriya Yoga.

do we, for the most part, feel abandoned and disconnected? Why is there such a stubborn silence from our Creator?

I admire great people such as Sri Ramakrishna[1], Swami Vivekananda, Sri Aurobindo[2], Paramahansa Yogananda[3] and many other sages who, through love, willpower and self-denial, were able to reach the heights of intuition. These beautiful souls were not ravaged by the gangrene that is all-powerful reason, which is today widespread in our schools and universities, as well as in our most sacred institutions. How can we escape the paralyzing, ruthless and cold grip that the intellect has on us and let the soul express itself? How can we, only for a moment, reach out to the part of us that is charitable, noble and immortal? Does the practice of shamanism with ayahuasca not deserve its place in this process?

❄ ❄ ❄

Up to this point of my life, I had never consumed any psychedelic substance. On the one hand, having strong analytical skills and being able to develop and express my thoughts clearly were

1. Ramakrishna Paramahansa (1836 – 1886) was an Indian mystic and yogi during the 19th century.

2. Sri Aurobindo (1872 – 1950) was an Indian philosopher, yogi, guru, poet, and nationalist. He joined the Indian movement for independence from British rule, for a while was one of its influential leaders and then became a spiritual reformer, introducing his visions on human progress and spiritual evolution.

3. Paramahansa Yogananda (1893 – 1952) was an Indian yogi and guru who introduced millions of Indians and westerners to the teachings of meditation and Kriya Yoga through his organization Yogoda Satsanga Society of India and Self-Realization Fellowship. His book, *Autobiography of a Yogi* remains a spiritual masterpiece and was included in the 100 best spiritual books of the 20th century.

the only tools I believed would allow me to progress in life. On the other hand, I was conscious of the legal ramifications of such practice in most countries. However, I had been feeling differently about ayahuasca and DMT for some time. The works[1] that I had read on the topic had taught me that similar substances were used by ancient societies in order to obtain very high levels of human consciousness.

While the idea of trying DMT in the near future had been in my thoughts for some time, I nevertheless had been waiting for the right moment. It seemed to me that such practice needed to be done with the sole intention to go beyond the boundaries of the intellect. Indulging in it for recreational purposes was out of the question. Ideally, I would have liked to be under the supervision of doctors or academics as part of a scientific or university study as described by Rick Strassman in his book *DMT: The Spirit Molecule*, but this seemed very unlikely.

Being able to take part in ayahuasca ceremonies in the Amazon jungle with Yogesh and Aesha under the direction and protection of shamans seemed too good an opportunity to miss.

---

1. Particularly the excellent book by Rick Strassman (1952—) *DMT, The Spirit Molecule*, as well as the book by Graham Hancock (1950—) *Supernatural: Meeting with the Ancient Teachers of Mankind*, and inevitably, the essential work of Aldous Huxley (1894—1963) *The Doors of Perception*.

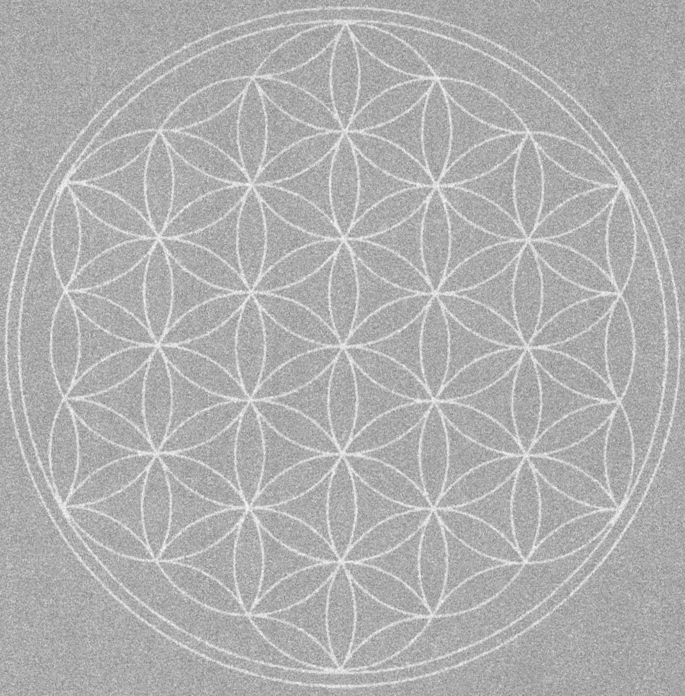

On the Amazon River

We can have in life but one great experience at best,
and the secret of life is to reproduce
that experience as often as possible.
—Oscar Wilde

November 3, 2016, Brasília, Brazil

At the counter of one the small shops at Brasília Airport, in the capital of Brazil, I felt someone put their hand on my shoulder.

"Hi, Adriano!"

That voice was familiar. I turned my head, it was Yogesh. He greeted me with a friendly hug and a broad smile, looking joyful. Very surprised to see him earlier than I had planned, I exclaimed:

"Yogesh! You, here! I can't believe that we are taking the same plane!"

"I know, it's incredible!"

"I'm very happy to see you here. Is Aesha with you?"

"Yes, she's sitting over there, with the suitcases."

I had not seen Yogesh or Aesha since the conversation in the little Italian restaurant in Dharamkot, a few weeks earlier. They had extended their stay at the intensive yoga retreat by three weeks, during which they were not allowed to access the Internet or their mobile phones. It was a great surprise to meet at this airport, waiting for the same plane to Rio Branco. This coincidence was going to be a source of cheerfulness between us during hard times to come.

I liked this couple a lot. Yogesh is from New Delhi, but he grew up in Goa, a small coastal town in Western India. Son of the owner of a very beautiful hotel and restaurant on the seaside, between his yoga and meditation retreats, Yogesh spends most of his time there working as the manager and excellent pizzaiolo. He is artistic, enjoys playing the guitar and, along with Aesha, often sings Hindu songs. He is always happy, even in difficult times. Our upcoming discussions will often be a source of joy and enthusiasm. Aesha was born in Kolkata, the largest city in East India and capital of West Bengal. She teaches mathematics at an elementary school in the center of the city. She travels to Goa and stay with Yogesh during school holidays. Like Yogesh, she always smiles. She is a calm and intuitive person. Her advice and attention will be very comforting to me during tough times in the jungle. Yogesh and Aesha found themselves perfectly. They show great kindness and inexhaustible patience.

Once we arrived in Rio Branco, the capital of the state of Acre, in North West Brazil, we met the other participants. In total, we were thirty-four people taking part in the shamanic festival. Veronica, an eighteen-year-old British girl, was the youngest of the group. William, a fifty-two-year-old, long-haired, Chinese-born New Yorker who looked like a Mexican gangster, was the oldest. I felt very comfortable amongst this eclectic and international group.

When some of them who took part in the festival the previous years saw each other, they hugged for a long time with a big grin on their face and cries of delight.

This was the third consecutive festival since its creation. Diego, a Brazilian man from Tarauacá, a small town in the state of Acre, was the creator. People related that a few years prior, after attending an ayahuasca ceremony in the village we were going to stay in, he had been so overwhelmed that he decided shortly thereafter to leave the comfort of Rio de Janeiro, where he owned a small guesthouse, to live part-time in the Amazon jungle. There, he created the first ayahuasca festival and has since taken it upon himself to promote it around the world. He then married the village chief shaman's beautiful daughter. When I met the charming couple for the first time, in Rio Branco, they had just had a very beautiful daughter.

In the evening, we congregated in a room next to the restaurant to introduce ourselves. When my turn came, I shared the fact that I had no experience in shamanism, and even less with ayahuasca. The fits of laughter as well as the comments from the other participants told me very clearly that I was either insane or unaware of the risks of starting my shamanic learning with such intense ceremonies, especially in the depths of the Amazon jungle. Perhaps they were right, but that did not stop me from taking part in their good spirits.

Early the next morning, we took the bus to Tarauacá, the final step before boarding on the Amazon River. The long road on the endless and battered dirt track was strenuous. After an eleven-hour journey, we finally reached our destination. We spent the night in a two-story hotel with two or three people per room.

The following day, I met Priscilla, a lovely Brazilian woman from Rio de Janeiro. Priscilla lived in France for a few years. Even though her English was pretty basic at the time, her grasp of the French language was impressive. Her voluminous light-brown hair, large sparkling and laughing black eyes, charming smile, as well as very feminine curves, attracted both men's and women's attention. I also met Hernan, an Argentine from Buenos Aires who was going to be sharing our boat on the Amazon River. Hernan is married to a Spanish woman and has lived in Spain for a few years on one of the Balearic Islands. He has been passionate about Japanese culture since childhood and has become a specialist in making sushi, maki, and sashimi. His dream is to open a small Japanese restaurant in Majorca, where he resides.

At dinner, in the spacious restaurant that occupied most of the small hotel's ground floor, Diego, his wife, the impressive chief shaman, and their assistants gave us the first instructions for the expedition on the river. It was also a good opportunity for us to know each other better. Everyone was really excited. We could not wait to embark.

The next day after breakfast, in small groups at a time, we climbed into the back of a small truck that transported us to the riverbank. We were then split onto six motorized boats. Our crew consisted of eight people: Yogesh, Aesha, Hernan, Priscilla, who also took the role of captain of our boat, our two operators Luiz and Gustavo, the cook Marcella, and me. Our wooden boats were six- or seven-meters long and about a meter and a half wide at the center. They were all topped by several thin vertical beams supporting a roof made of three or four wooden battens, covered by a plastic tarp added on in a perfunctory manner. There was not a lot of room to move on board once the bags and suitcases had been stacked in the middle of the boat. In order to get from one end to the other, we had to skillfully zigzag between the bags, suitcases, and supplies while ducking to avoid hitting the head-high horizontal beams. The provisions and a hob made of four firebricks in the shape of a square were stored at the front of the boat. There were already glowing embers in the middle of the hob when we embarked; Marcella had already started to prepare breakfast.

We had to wait for hours before we could leave the shore. The boat owners and organizers were constantly running between our vessels and the small shops located some fifty meters away. There was always something missing. The boat drivers finally raised the anchors, pushed the boats to free them from the grip of the sand, and in one jump sat down next to the engines. We showed our delight with cries of happiness. The moment we had been waiting for had finally arrived.

Our boats aligned quickly, each about thirty meters away from the next. We stopped, had lunch, and dined all together in the same places. We sailed from sunrise to sunset without stopping. We spent the nights in hammocks hooked diagonally to the roof's vertical structures, or to the posts of a hut in a village along the river. The meals, mainly consisting of white rice, spaghetti, beans, corns, and bananas, were prepared by Marcella at the front of the boat and eaten on a sand beach along the river. We sometimes shared our provisions taken from the town to interrupt the monotony of the meals prepared with the limited ingredients available on board.

The constant roar from the engine at the back of the boat was so loud that we had to communicate with gestures, looks, and smiles. We spent our days on the boat looking at the beautiful landscapes that renewed themselves at each of the river's countless bends, listening to music with earbuds pushed firmly in our ears, reading, playing chess, or dozing off. When the sunlight became too weak for us to sail safely, we stopped for the night. Every time the boat hit the sandbank, I quickly jumped off and wondered if I was happier because dinner was going to be promptly served or because of the sudden silence after the engine stopped. Once the boats were anchored and ready to be used as dormitories, a few beautiful souls grabbed their guitars and other musical instruments to sing and celebrate around a small wood fire.

We were constantly attacked by an incredible number of sand fleas. They were so tiny that we could barely see them. Unfortunately, our insecticides and other lotions did not have much effect on them. From the second day, any part of the body that had been exposed to air was covered in bites that itched horribly. For some of us and later in the village, the bites were infected to such an extent that they had to take antibiotics to heal them. Despite the torrid heat and humidity, we had to wear long pants, long-sleeved T-shirts, scarves and hats until we returned a whole month later. It was practically impossible to walk or bathe in the river without being surrounded by an army of starving insects. Nevertheless, some of us, including me, took a daily morning bath in the river using biodegradable soap. We had to bathe very quickly to minimize the number of insect bites.

The river level was unusually low for the season. The organizers of our expedition were eagerly awaiting the rain. We had to push the boats out of the sand more than once. With our feet in the murky water and in the mud up to our ankles, we were afraid to get bitten by a snake, walk on a stingray, or be attacked by one of the countless creatures living in the river. On last year's return journey, a participant had inadvertently stepped on a stingray. We were told that it was not serious, but he suffered horribly for three days, which was very reassuring!

After two days on the river, we were seriously worried because the water level kept going down. On several occasions, the boat drivers had to create a path with blades and chainsaws in order to sail between the massive tree trunks that had fallen across the river. They had been transported by the current and were stacked in the places where the water level was at its lowest, making an impenetrable wall, even for our relatively small boats. We were told many times that if the river level continued to decrease, we would have to stop the expedition and wait for the rain, or in the worst-case scenario, go back to Tarauacá. Much to our relief, it ended up pouring with rain for two nights and one day.

Even though we were not allowed to bathe in the river, I dove in every time the boat reached land. The fresh water relieved my insect bites and refreshed my body. I would only get out after getting tired from fighting the current or when the meal was served. Yogesh, Hernan, sometimes Aesha, and I often ran happily and hastily to about a hundred meters above the river to throw ourselves in and return to the boat with the strong current. Priscilla was worried to see us in the turbulent water and scowled at us, hoping that we would return to the shore. She was so pretty when she pouted that we could not help but smile at her, before jumping into the water again.

Marcella, our head chef, was a native Amazonian woman. She lived in a small village along the river. She was an excellent cook. On several occasions between meals, she painted our faces, backs, and arms with shamanic patterns. That is the custom in this part of the Amazon. On the fourth day, we stopped for a few hours in her native village. As we just passed the last bend of the river that separated us from the village, we noticed a number of people waiting for us on the bank. They must have heard the noise of the engines from afar. Some children were playing in the water, others were just on the bank and making signs in our direction. As soon as the boat berthed, Yogesh, Aesha, Hernan, and I threw ourselves into the water to refresh ourselves. The children still on the bank did the same. They laughed joyfully and had a great time. When we motioned for them to come closer to us, they immersed themselves completely to hide their shyness, then reappeared at the other side of the boat or on the other bank. We tried to catch them, but they were so agile in the river's turbulent waters that none of us ever succeeded. We enjoyed playing with the children that afternoon. Their big smiles, innocence and bright looks full of life will stay etched in my memory.

We shared a meal with Marcella's family inside a large hut made of wood and straw, which was a unique and very special moment. Before saying goodbye, Priscilla and Marcella gave biscuits to the children, as well as rice and corn to the adults.

We boarded our boats with light hearts, full of joy, and continued our journey on the river.

November 12, 2016, Nova Futura, the Amazon, Brazil

We reached our destination in the middle of the fifth afternoon. The river level was one to two meters lower than it should have been during this season. About a hundred meters before mooring, we heard a song accompanied by the noise of drums, which triggered great joy on board. As soon as our boat reached the bank, a handful of villagers hurried to take our belongings and carried them to our hut. A small group of a dozen people, mainly young women and children covered in strange ornaments and multicolored paintings, raced down the slope towards us while singing at the top of their lungs, then took our hands and ran with us to a large straw hut in the center of the village. In the evening, I was to learn that this hut, called 'the maloca', was the village's sacred place where the shamanic ayahuasca ceremonies were going to take place. We followed the villagers' circle dance for a while inside the maloca. I was amazed by the amount of beauty and life that oozed from them. A joie de vivre and sincerity that no longer exist in our big cities emanated from their sparkling eyes and broad smiles. The participants who arrived just after us on the other boats were treated to the same warm welcome.

We had, finally, reached our destination.

Our accommodations were simple wooden stilt huts, about a meter off the ground and covered by a slanted straw roof. Our hut had two rooms separated by a thin wooden wall. Yogesh, Aesha, and I shared the room directly at the entrance. Hernan and Priscilla took the room at the back of the hut. We wasted no time unpacking our bags that took up all of the free space on the little rack near the entrance and the two little benches placed along the windows.

We then unfurled our hammocks and mosquito nets and attached them to the horizontal beams on the hut's roof. Finally, we set up our small tents just next to the hammocks.

Every year, the organizers, a group of volunteers, and the villagers gathered to improve the village's living conditions. The first year, they built a large hut about ten meters away from the maloca which is now used as the canteen. The year that followed, solar panels were installed to power small lamps and other small electrical devices which were becoming more and more common in the village. This year, ecological toilets had been put in place in each of the four corners of the campsite before we arrived, as well as four shower cubicles powered by elevated reservoirs filled manually with water from the river. The organizers were more than thrilled with these new facilities.

It was finally time for our meal. We were extremely relieved that we would not have to endure the boat's uncomfortable conditions anymore and gathered around long tables in the canteen to share our first meal with the shamans, the organizers, and some of the villagers.

❄ ❄ ❄

Nova Futura is a medium-sized village. It is the last village along the river to be visited by our modern civilizations. Tribes that stubbornly refuse contact with our world live a little deeper in the forest. It is said that some of their inhabitants fire arrows at planes in the sky with their wooden bows and threaten to kill any stranger who has the audacity to tread on their property. Many other amusing and worrying stories go around. I have never met these tribes, but the stories about them are picturesque, to say the least.

Our village is inhabited by the Huni Kuin people (pronounced, 'hu-knee queen'), which means 'the True People'. Ninawa is the chief and shaman of the village. A deep peace and great love emanate from his authentic smile. Contrary to popular belief, which is that shamans are wizards living in a world of myths and legends, the actual truth is completely different. In order to accomplish the tasks they are burdened with—healing, divination, etc., shamans enter a trance state where they acquire the ability to operate simultaneously in the living and spirit worlds. A shaman is a being that has a deep understanding of the different states of consciousness that govern the physical and spiritual realms. In order to become a shaman, the candidate, who is most often designated during their childhood by an experienced shaman, must survive a very tough education. Very few manage to overcome the countless challenges that they face throughout their life. Even fewer gain an honorable reputation. In the community, the shaman often takes on the role of healer. Their vast knowledge of the forest, plants, spirits, as well as the world of the dead, would make most of our doctors—even the most qualified ones—speechless. When the shaman is in a normal state of consciousness (as opposed to a trance state), they are a very pragmatic being who takes on the role of village leader. It is not uncommon for them to fish, hunt, and go about all of the other important daily tasks for the life and survival of the community. Even though most shamans are men, it is possible to meet excellent female shamans.

❋ ❋ ❋

"Other shamans will join Ninawa during the ceremonies. And there will be no fewer than eight!" Bernard, one of the participants, told me. "The more shamans, the more benevolent spirits amongst us, and the more we will be protected from evil spirits!" he continued.

Even though Bernard's expression was full of enthusiasm and was an invitation to learn more, I felt that it was too much information to handle at the time. I decided not to question my friend. I thought that in any case, this world was so foreign to me that I was going to wait for the evening's ceremony to see it with my own eyes.

I could not wait to begin.

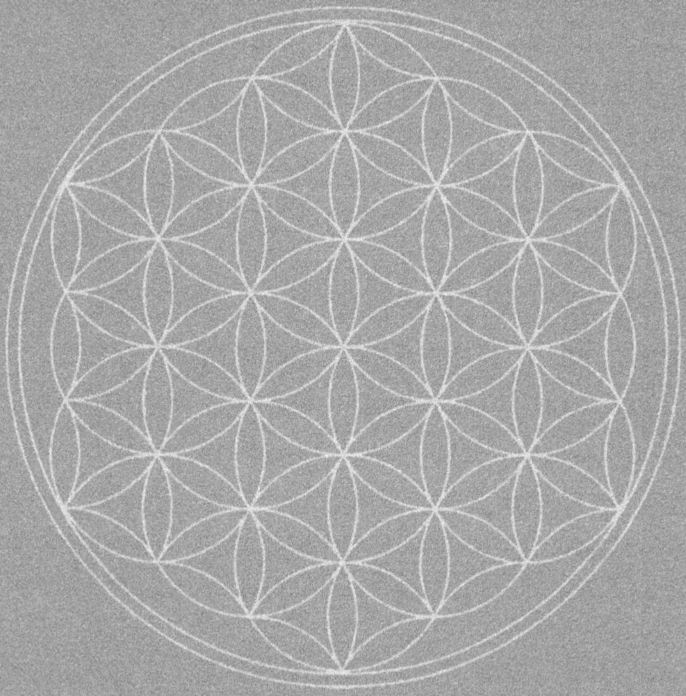

Sacred Geometry

The important and beautiful thing about geometry is that, through its purity, it is an instrument of thought.
— Paul Valéry

November 12, 2016

It was ten o'clock at night and pitch black outside. We were all gathered around a small wood fire in the middle of the large ceremonial hut, the maloca. Each of the participants had very carefully arranged their sacred items on a small rug or on a scarf spread out on the sand, towards the purifying fire. Amongst those items were feather headdresses, rattles, flasks, smoking pipes, feathers of different kinds, sizes, and colors, multicolored pearl bracelets, tie-shaped necklaces decorated with geometric symbols, and many other totems and talismans, each more bizarre than the next. Every aspect, color, shape, and object had its own particular function to move along the different levels of consciousness or to ensure divine protection, but I was to discover that later. As I did not know what was appropriate to use during the ceremonies, I did not bring anything with me. I could barely recognize some of my friends. In addition to their phantasmagorical tunics, they had painted their face, hands, arms, and all of the other visible parts of their body with extravagant patterns. They were beautiful, for they exuded a certain nobility.

The shamans, who were dressed in long ceremonial tunics and wearing imposing, multicolored feather headdresses, had already taken their place on the small wooden chairs at the back of the maloca, opposite the entrance. Ninawa, the chief shaman, was standing. He was wearing a larger, taller and more impressive feather headdress than his fellow shamans. A wooden statuette painted with geometric patterns, freshly picked flowers, and a recipient which apparently contained the ayahuasca were placed on a small wooden table in front of him. There was absolute silence. Everyone was waiting for the shaman to open the ceremony, to open the festival. When he finally broke the silence with his deep voice to welcome us, we applauded and cheered with delight. The other shamans and villagers happily joined in. Ninawa's presence was imposing and reassuring. He radiated a calm strength and infinite kindness. It was obvious that everyone had great respect and love for the being that he was. When he spoke, everyone listened carefully. After a relatively short welcoming speech, he invited us to form a line in front of the small wooden table on which the ayahuasca recipient was standing.

I was anxious. Before standing up, I looked at Bernard, who was sitting beside me. Bernard is Canadian and approaching his forties. He used to be a project manager at an IT company in Toronto. After working sixty-five hours a week on average for fifteen years, he left his job to become a full-time artist. He now writes poetry, plays, as well as scripts and stories for Canadian television channels.

When I met him at the festival, he had just won a national poetry award. Even if Bernard is not a veteran in terms of shamanism and ayahuasca yet, he seems to have significant experience based on the discussions that we had in Tarauacá.

"Bernie… I think that now is the time…" I told him while looking at him with half a smile.

"Ha-ha, my friend. Yes, now is *your* time. Oh, brother… I can't wait for you to tell me all about it tomorrow. I am sure that you will find it *interesting*. Good luck!" he told me while tapping my shoulder.

"Yes… Tell me, Bernie, one more thing… Can you give me one last bit of advice before I stand up and join the queue for the ayahuasca?" I asked him with a slightly nervous smile.

"Ah, yes… Listen to me carefully, what I am about to tell you is important. Ayahuasca has an unfortunate tendency to trigger a strong and irresistible desire to vomit, and that happens to everyone after about an hour or two. It sometimes happens straight after drinking!" Bernard guffawed while throwing himself slightly backwards. Leaning forward again, he put on a serious face and continued, "I can tell you that it is not funny, brother. However, there is worse. Some people get diarrhea and are incapable of controlling themselves because of the crippling effect that ayahuasca can have. They do it in their pants! Listen carefully, though. Whatever happens, try with all of your might not to vomit in the maloca. If you do end up doing in your pants, take a shower, change your clothes, and come back quickly."

I had learned about ayahuasca's notorious emetic and purgative effects while reading some of the shamanic literature, but strangely enough, up until that point, I had not realized that it could concern me directly, and that, in the very near future. While feverishly staring at the roof of the maloca above me, I was hoping with all of my heart that I would not be part of the second category of people that Bernard had just described.

It took me a lot of courage to get in the line. My apprehension was due to what I had recently read regarding the effects of this fearsome brew. All of it was now coming back to me: vomiting, diarrhea, loss of control of faculties, temporary loss of memory, and other undesirable effects were described by most of those who had taken the same path. I also wondered what I was going to see during the inevitable visions, and I was terrified of my own reaction to them. I was simply afraid of the unknown.

I eventually summoned up the courage and took my place in the line, then patiently waited my turn.

"You can still go back if you want ... or wait for the next ceremony," I told myself, several times. My heart was racing. I took a deep breath. However, even though I was no longer convinced of the reason for this foolish adventure, I was also very curious to know what the vine of the dead—or the key which opens the door to the spirit world—had in store for me. I moved in the line mechanically, step by step, looking at the sandy ground, lost in thought. Suddenly, I found myself face to face with Ninawa, the impressive shaman. It was too late to turn back now, even if I had wanted to. The chief shaman stared at me for a moment with his penetrating gaze, then placed a small glass next to the bottle containing the ayahuasca which had a small tap at its base. When he opened it, a black liquid poured out. Once the glass was full, he carefully closed the plastic tap, took the glass with both hands, and held it out to me. There was no noise in the maloca. Only the small crackling sounds of the fire behind were breaking the silence with care. For a few moments, I felt that time had slowed down. The air became rare. I then realized that I did not know the tradition: did I have to salute the shaman, make a particular gesture? Did I have to thank him, say something? I looked into his eyes, then slightly lowered my head as a sign of respect. His solemn expression, due to his imposing feather headdress, suddenly relented when he smiled at me, which was reassuring. I grabbed the glass with both hands, lowered my head again out of respect, and then smiled at the shaman.

Before drinking ayahuasca, it is strongly recommended to set a positive intention for the upcoming ceremony. This is intimately linked to the participant's desire. It can be the need to acquire material possessions, improve a relationship or situation, or get answers to pressing questions.

My intention was clear: "Thank you, Divine Spirits, for letting me explore the spiritual worlds and for protecting me during this ceremony." I drank the contents of the glass without pausing. The taste was surprisingly pleasant. It reminded me of certain Chinese plant-based medicinal decoctions that I was used to, having lived in China a long time. Besides that, it had a light aftertaste of orange and sweet alcohol. When I returned to my seat—which was my yoga mat—I told Bernard that the taste was unexpectedly enjoyable. He gave me a big smile and murmured: "See, ayahuasca already likes you!" I closed my eyes, then meditated with my legs crossed in the half-lotus position and observed any changes in me, quite anxiously.

I have absolutely no recollection of what happened immediately after that other than an extreme difficulty to think and an irresistible desire to sleep. I surely lost consciousness because the only memories that I have today are those that came just before the second glass of ayahuasca, which is normally three to four hours after taking the first serving.

When I opened my eyes, I did not know that so much time had passed. I felt completely normal. Thinking that I had only closed my eyes for a brief moment, I sat up and, when I saw my friends lining up for their second glass, I felt sad because I thought that ayahuasca had no effect on me, as is the case for one in ten people[1]. "What will I try after ayahuasca if it has no effect on me?" I thought, concerned. Just as I did the first time, I waited in line behind the other participants. When my turn came, Ninawa held the glass to me and smiled again. For some reason, his expression seemed strange, almost worrying.

I returned to my mat and meditated. After a while, I felt extremely nauseous. I stood up and took the direction to the toilets so I would not vomit in the maloca. I had only just walked out of the hut when I realized I was so intoxicated that I could not walk straight, just like after drinking heavily. I could barely stand on my legs. It was pitch black outside. The sky was slightly starry. The contrast between the white sand path under my feet and the dark and dense jungle made the setting gloomy and impressive. When I reached a tree to the left of the maloca, I tightly grabbed the trunk with both hands to regain balance, then looked up to take a deep breath.

1. Widely reported, but different sources report different figures.

To my great surprise, I saw that each of the leaves above my head had taken the shape of triangles that were vibrating to the rhythm of the music from inside the maloca. I was stunned. I lowered my head, looked at the ground, and realized that each footprint left in the sand had taken the same shape and was also beating to the rhythm of the music. I slowly turned my head to look around me and was staggered to see that *everything* around me was made up of these strange animated triangular shapes.

The nausea was worsening, I needed to find somewhere to vomit, quickly. A few steps away, between two trees, I leaned forward, stood my feet apart, opened my mouth, lowered my head, and made a few back and forth movements with my stomach to empty it. Nothing came out. When I looked up, I saw a scene entirely made up of triangles depicting a dark, gloomy, and worrying jungle in front of me. "Gosh… A swamp!" I mentally shouted while taking a few steps back. "Come to your senses… Find the toilets," I continued. Through reading about ayahuasca, I knew that the visions could sometimes be terrifying, and that you had to remain calm and never venture into the forest alone. I came back to my senses and tried to find my way to the toilets. At that point, the whole setting was made up of little triangles that were vibrating to the rhythm of the music. As it was very dark, it was almost impossible for me to make sense of the images that were appearing before my eyes. I felt more and more intoxicated. I would take a step to the right, then to the left, then a step back, and a few steps forward, all while trying to walk in one direction.

A few meters away, I saw a light coming from a small wooden cabin in the distance. "The toilets," I shouted. After a long and perilous climb, I entered the cabin, but despite all of my efforts, I was unable to vomit. I spent a long while lost in my thoughts then reemerged. During the group meeting the day before, the organizers told us to always stay close to the maloca. However, at that moment, I was unable to find my way back. It was very dark all around me. It was also extremely challenging to regain control of my faculties and almost impossible to think clearly. A villager wearing a tall headdress ran past me as quickly as he could and disappeared into one of the two wooden cabins. He somehow gave me the courage to try again. While I could clearly hear the noises made by my neighbor's efforts to vomit, I did not succeed in doing the same. I decided to give up and leave the toilets. The man with the imposing feather headdress left the cabin and disappeared in the forest as quickly as he had appeared. My vision was blurred, as if my eyes were unable to see more than one or two images per second.

Suddenly, as if by magic, Asil, one of the veterans of ayahuasca ceremonies, appeared before me. He was dressed in white from head to toe. Contrary to the setting that looked full of triangles beating to the rhythm of the music, Asil's face was steady and surprisingly bright. He gave me a big smile. I then felt he was going to tell me something. With a lot of effort, I managed to focus my attention on his face. I saw him open his mouth and start to move his lips in slow motion. I knew he was talking, but no sound was reaching my ears. Then, with considerable delay and an abnormally long pause between each word, he said:

"It … would … be … wiser … to…"

I could not hear anything after that. Time stopped. Another voice interjected and added:

"Follow … the … light."

Then, I heard Asil's voice again:

"Go … back … to … your … seat."

I was stupefied. I knew that my friend had told me: "It would be wiser to go back to your seat," but I was sure that the message that I was meant to receive was: "It would be wiser to follow the light." My friend vanished as suddenly as he had appeared.

It was vital that I return to the maloca because I had read in a book describing the effects of ayahuasca that participants were often imprisoned mentally—hence physically—in one place, and that place was very often the toilets. I was terrified by that thought. A small, dimly lit path appeared before me. "This must be the way back," I exclaimed loudly. I decided to follow it, slowly, putting one foot in front of the other, while doing my best to keep balance. After what felt like an eternity, I arrived at a small mound of land from which a perpendicular path intersected. I did not know which way to follow. Everything was dark because the light coming from the wooden cabin was far behind me. I was lost again. "I should go back to the toilets…" I sadly concluded. Scott, another veteran of ayahuasca ceremonies, told me that if I happened to be lost, I would need to take a few deep breaths to come back to my senses, which I did several times, but in vain. Suddenly, I saw a woman wearing an exceptionally bright white blouse that was leaving a long and phosphorescent track as she passed by. The words: "It would be wiser to follow the light" came back to me. I smiled and followed the light which eventually brought me to the maloca. Though it was dark outside and there were no signs of life on the horizon, the atmosphere inside the ceremonial hut was lively and full of music. I did not really understand what was happening because everything was going far too fast for my untrained eyes.

When I reached my mat, I let my body collapse to the floor. Lying on my back and as soon as my eyelids closed, I saw a myriad of forms appear before me, like a gigantic firework invading all of the space. An array of geometric shapes and colors of such magnificence that was unknown to me up to that point relentlessly appeared and disappeared, one after the other, progressing from earth to sky, left to right, and front to back. I could not believe my eyes.

After some time, they suddenly transformed into protruding spikes covered in bright red and green. "Oh! I don't like this," I shouted in my mind. They instantaneously transformed into a harmonious parade of geometric shapes, quicker than it had taken me to express that thought. "Oh! I can do that…" I continued, stunned. The celestial battle that was taking place before my eyes seemed to be in perfect harmony with the music playing in the maloca. A music note generated a shape, the next gave it sparkling colors, the following made it vibrate, and yet another note gave it life and unbounded freedom.

After watching the dazzling performance for what seemed like an eternity, I opened my eyes to realize that everything around me was beating to the rhythm of the music. The roof of the maloca was made of long and thin wooden battens on which dried up banana tree leaves were placed transversely. The parts of the leaves between the battens had now taken on the appearance of small living beings dancing to the rhythm of the music. Even though they were following the same melody, each of them was doing its own dance and seemed to have its own existence. In a state of bliss and amazed by this exceptional parade, I watched the celestial dancers almost one by one. In rows of thousands, like countless figurines inhabiting the murals of the Hindu god, Shiva, they radiated happiness. They were beautiful. They seemed free. They looked immensely happy.

I started to feel ill again. I decided to go back to the toilets. Like the first time, it was an arduous journey. I could not vomit. I went a total of five times, but to no avail. During the last try, on the way back to the maloca, I saw one of the female participants. She stopped in front of me and stared at me with abnormally big eyes and extraordinary beauty. "Avatar," I exclaimed in my mind while taking half a step back. "She really exists… She's so beautiful!" She inexplicably looked like the main female character of the film in question. I stared at her for a moment then smiled. She touched my shoulder and gave me a big smile in return, then told me something. I saw her lips move but could not understand what she was saying. I wanted to take her in my arms, but I was unable to move, for everything around me was moving. I felt like I was standing on a boat being shaken by storm. I then quickly made my way back to the solid ground of the maloca.

I lay on my back, closed my eyes while breathing a long and deep sigh. With my eye still shut, I saw my entire body vibrate to the music while disintegrating into thousands of colored bubbles and replenishing immediately after. It felt as if a large snake had taken control of my body from head to toe and, at the same time, a bright electric discharge went through my spine, from my feet to the top of my skull. During this process, it was as if the electric flow which accompanied each of the snake's waves was purifying me deep inside. These sensations and visions seemed to last an eternity. I eventually lost consciousness.

❋ ❋ ❋

When I reopened my eyes, everything around me looked normal again. The effects of ayahuasca had faded. The ceremony had ended and the sun was rising.

Before walking back to my hut, Cathie, a young British woman, and I went for a walk to the top of the hill just behind the campsite. From there, we gazed at the panorama that was partially lit by the rays of the rising sun. The scene resembled a surreal painting in vivid and warm colors depicting the tireless and winding flow of the waters of a broad river running through the dense and lush vegetation of the Amazon. We stayed there for a long time without saying a word.

Once the jungle was entirely lit up, I went to my hut and slept soundly.

❋ ❋ ❋

Later, at breakfast, some of the participants shared their adventures from the night before. Bernard wanted to know about my first taste of ayahuasca. He and some of the other people sitting at our table burst out laughing when I told them how I had fallen asleep without realizing the time that had elapsed between the first and second glasses of ayahuasca, how I had met the beautiful Avatar, and the many trips to the toilets.

Even if I had a thousand questions about what happened during the ceremony, I decided not to delve deeper. I thought that engaging analysis and reasoning in this process would have only destroyed the beauty and magic of the events that were still so fresh in my mind. However, there was one question that was haunting me more than the others. During my visions, and more particularly when I had my eyes closed and was completely absorbed by the phantasmagorical spectacle, I had the indescribable feeling that time had been distorted. It was difficult, perhaps impossible for me to quantify this phenomenon because I had no reference point to do so. However, most experiences seemed to last very long, abnormally long. I mentioned this to Asil, who confirmed that time is very often warped when under the influence of ayahuasca or other psychedelic substances. According to my friend, some accounts mention phenomenally long periods of time, feeling as if days, weeks, months, and even years have passed, even though only a few minutes or hours had gone by in reality.

At the end of the afternoon, I felt full of joy and wholly satisfied. I was already looking forward to the upcoming evening ceremony.

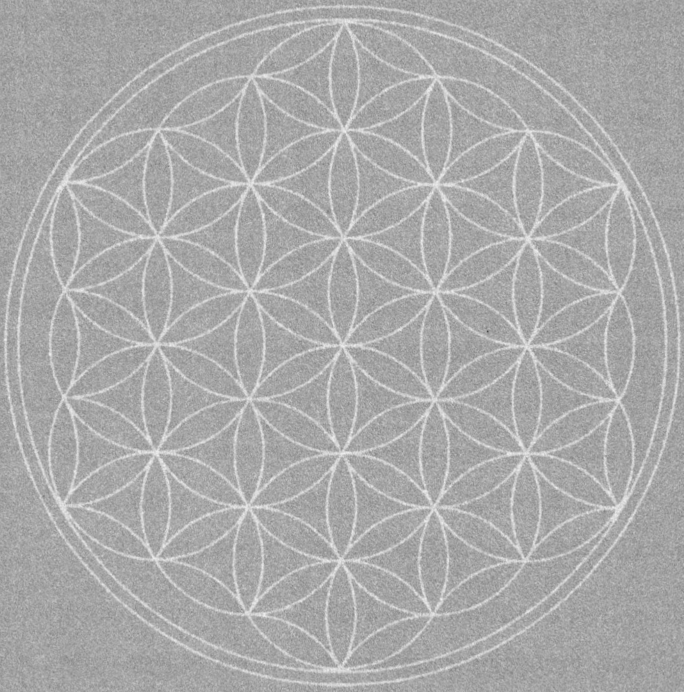

The Power of Sound

Music is the language of emotions.
— Emmanuel Kant

November 13, 2016

I was not particularly nervous before the second ceremony. After what I had experienced the night before, I was relatively calm. I was wondering, however, if I was going to encounter the multi-colored visions again.

While holding out the glass of ayahuasca to me, Ninawa smiled, like he did the night before. Even though his expression seemed somehow a little strange to me, I thought that it was a good omen he smiled each time. The ayahuasca tasted of a mixture of plants and an aftertaste of orange and sweet alcohol, like the night before. Without wandering in my thoughts, I turned around, took a few steps, and sat in one of the corners of the maloca to reflect on my intention. Just as I did during the first ceremony, I asked for the ayahuasca spirit to take me through spiritual worlds and to protect me during the night.

Unlike the first ceremony, however, I did not lose sense of time shortly after drinking the first glass of ayahuasca. I remained conscious, sitting cross-legged, in the half-lotus position. I observed each sensation and listened to every sound. After about fifteen minutes, I noticed that they became exceptionally amplified. Every murmur and every whisper seemed to be abnormally close to my ears. Every crackling of the fire felt like sharp and loud explosions which filled the entire space. I then eagerly awaited the stronger effects of the ayahuasca for what felt like an eternity. I feared that nothing was going to happen. "I am surely too nervous. Perhaps I should relax," I thought, anxiously. I breathed deeply for a few long minutes.

Suddenly, the sounds in the maloca became even louder. The noises made by the participants rubbing their clothes at the other end of the maloca became so intense that I heard them resonating in my ears. Our slow breaths filled the maloca. The experience of the previous ceremony came back to me. Somehow mechanically, I raised my hands to my eyes and saw my fingertips evaporating in smoke as if they were being swept away by a light breeze. "Oh… It's starting…" I said with amazement. My journey had indeed begun.

My eyes still open, I saw geometrical shapes forming on the maloca's straw walls. Colors became more and more vivid. After watching the parade for a few minutes, I felt overwhelmingly tired, so much so that I became incapable of resisting the temptation to lie down. With great effort, I grabbed with both hands a small and abnormally heavy cushion to my right, dragged it behind me, and collapsed on my mat. After a few awkward movements to lie flat on my back, stretch my legs and lie down my arms, my eyelids shut.

Immediately afterwards, I became submerged by extremely intense visions. On the far horizon, a succession of geometrical shapes appeared, expanded, shrank, and disappeared in an endless cycle. They were adorned with an array of vivid and bright colors. The shapes seemed to follow an underlying flow as if animated by the calm waters of a large river in a slow, circular, and almost repetitive motion. There was no music in the maloca. Absolute silence reigned amongst the shamans, which surprised me. "Oh... This is the part I missed yesterday," I thought, "between the first and second servings of ayahuasca".

After a few minutes, the shapes suddenly took life and rapidly filled the vast sky like they had been pushed by the violent and sudden explosions of a giant firework. They continued to multiply endlessly, forming a swarm of aggressive and sharp spikes moving in unison, rending and tearing the horizon apart. They were red and green of an exceptionally high intensity. The shamanic chants had just begun. In a very peculiar manner, the incantations seemed to orchestrate the shapes and colors. Each sound that came from the shamans injected strength and vitality into the battalion of disturbing shapes. Thousands of spikes joined together to form a single group that navigated the sky from side to side, then separated and regrouped in a never-ending cycle. Contrary to the previous ceremony, I did not try to influence the procession. Even if its grandeur and magnificence were somehow terrifying, I was awestruck by its infinite beauty.

Most of the other participants were also lying down, their heads about a meter away from the straw wall which separated us from the outdoors. Our feet were pointed towards the fire in the center of the maloca. From where I was, about a meter or two away outside of the maloca I could hear through the straw wall one of the participants vomiting. I had the disturbing feeling that he was vomiting on me. I decided to change position and have my head pointing towards the fire. I closed my eyes again. The disturbing feeling went away, but the multicolored, explosive and worrying visions came back. When I opened my eyes again, I saw a few people dancing around the fire. My eyelids shut again shortly after under the dizzying and intoxicating effect of the concoction and the fatigue. Everything went dark as I passed out.

When I regained consciousness, the battle of projected shapes had ended. An entirely different setting had taken its place. A gigantic labyrinth adorned with dazzling bright lights was floating above me. Suspended in the sky, it filled the entire horizon. Even though it was immobile, inside, life was flowing with great intensity. A fluorescent green liquid was pumped with powerful force into its lanes. In the maloca, the shamanic chants had made way for harmonious music. The shamans and villagers, accompanied by their guitars and drums, were singing their favorite song at the top of their lungs. That is when I became fully aware of the importance of sound during ayahuasca ceremonies.

The life that inhabited the enormous labyrinth and what was happening inside of me seemed to be inextricably linked. Each musical note injected a powerful new wave of liquid in the lanes of the labyrinth and, at the same time, generated an electric shock that went through my entire body, from feet to head, as if I was one of the strings of an immense celestial instrument. This feeling was perhaps comparable to an orgasm experienced by my entire body over an extraordinarily long period of time. It alternately gave me intense pleasure and pain. I felt, probably for the first time in my life, that I was part of a whole that was fundamentally perfect. I had the strong impression that I was at the source of life.

This experience seemed to last for hours. It was interrupted by pauses from when the music stopped. During these interludes, the light in the labyrinth dimmed, its colors darkened and lost their vitality. Through my shut eyelids, I saw the glow coming from the embers in the center of the maloca. I wondered why the colorful visions had to stop when the music ceased. I then challenged myself to test my mental abilities. I decided to revive them. From the faint glow coming from the embers, I mentally injected light into them so they could take a defined shape. Without too much effort, I succeeded in transforming them into a circle, then a sphere, and a succession of shapes each more complex than the last. I gave them a golden and sparkling color with disconcerting ease. That way, I could create many more complex shapes. Even though they were lively, they never had the intensity, vitality, and incomparable beauty of the great labyrinth. Nevertheless, I was infinitely satisfied and amazed by this new possibility.

When the music started again, the labyrinth reappeared. The golden shapes stayed in the foreground for a few moments before fading and completely disappearing. Every time the music stopped, I did the same mental exercise with growing ease. At some point, I noticed that a chain of complex shapes that I had just created looked like a town seen from above. Then, an extraordinarily bright city appeared before my astonished eyes, and in my mind, I was able to travel across the sky and cross over magnificent and luminous constructions.

When the ceremony ended, I was convinced, without a shadow of a doubt, of the paramount importance of sound in the experience of anyone under the influence of ayahuasca. In some ways, I knew it was the framework of the shamanic experience. I then wondered what could have happened if the music had never started, or worse, if it was dissonant.

Several times during the ceremony, I watched the shamans sing tirelessly and the villagers and some participants dance around the fire until the early hours of the morning. Knowing that they had also consumed ayahuasca, I could not help but be impressed by their energy and strength given that I had spent the night lying on the floor, powerless, incapable of moving, let alone standing up and dancing.

❄ ❄ ❄

When I woke up the next day, I was euphoric and satisfied with my experience the night prior. It seemed unreal to me. I was convinced that I had seen perfection. Yet, even though these visions were extraordinary and interesting, I realized that I still had not learned anything about myself or the spiritual world that surrounds us. I somehow feared that each ceremony would be the same. I mentioned this to Scott, a participant who was very experienced with ayahuasca. He told me that I had to see beyond the shapes by looking in the center of them to understand their message or meaning. He added that if an evil-looking entity emerged, I would have to look straight into its eyes without flinching. He further added that even if it looked monstrous, it could be beneficial to the observer and, the only way to be certain of that would be to look straight into its eyes.

"If it looks away when you stare at it, it's probably because it wants to hurt you," said Scott. "From that moment, it will take you mental strength to push it away. You will have to do this peacefully, without fear or violence. If you are scared, it will feed on your fear to become even more terrifying."

As I had not encountered any nightmarish visions thus far, I could not really understand my friend's advice regarding self-control in the face of fear. I would have to wait for the next ceremony to fully understand his wise words.

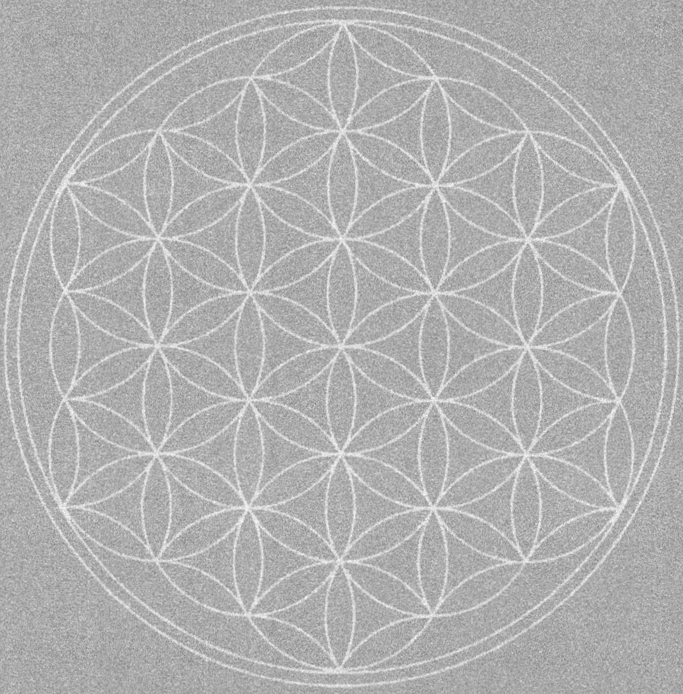

The Ruthless Game of the Ego

The ego is what stops people from being equal.
—Claude Frisoni

November 15, 2016

This ceremony was to take place under a full moon. According to my friends, the moon was to be the brightest it had been for the past seventy years. "There will be a supermoon[1] tonight!" they all exclaimed with a nervous smile. Everyone was wary, including the Huni Kuins, which surprised me. Given that my previous experiences with ayahuasca had been filled with beauty and harmony, logic dictated that I would have nothing to worry about that night. However, I was anxious. I feared the unknown. Furthermore, unlike the first two ceremonies that took place in the maloca, this one was to be outside, under the glow of the full moon. This decision worried me even more because it seemed obvious to me that we would have been more comfortable, and safe, in a confined space under a roof.

---

1. A new moon that approximately coincides with the closest distance that the Moon reaches to Earth in its elliptic orbit, resulting in a larger-than-usual apparent size of the lunar disk as seen from Earth.

At the agreed time, we gathered at the outskirts of the maloca to make a large circle around the wood fire. I unrolled my yoga mat on the sand and sat along the circle path. The moon had not appeared yet, it was pitch black. Once the shamans had taken their seats, ayahuasca was served. When my turn came, Ninawa smiled broadly as he held out the glass with both hands to me. For a reason that I could not comprehend, his expression disturbed me. Uncontrollable thoughts and doubts went through my mind: "Am I making a big mistake by taking part in *this* ceremony? Ninawa is surely wondering why I am doing something so absurd…" I thought. "What are you doing here? These ceremonies are not for you. Drink this glass and you will suffer the bitter consequences," he probably was trying to warn me silently, through his enigmatic smile. I was confused because I knew that Ninawa was a wise and kind man. How could this ceremony be any different to the previous ones that he had held? In order to have a clear conscience, I decided to watch the participants in front of me when ayahuasca is served during the next ceremony.

After drinking the content of the glass, I immediately felt nauseous. I took a few steps to the right to quickly leave the queue. I had to breathe deeply for a few long minutes in order to not vomit. The mild orange and alcoholic fragrance had been replaced with a horribly bitter and viscous texture.

I went back to my yoga mat, sat in the half-lotus position, and started to meditate. My intention for this ceremony was the same as for the previous nights: explore the spiritual realms under the protection of celestial spirits.

After about twenty minutes, I felt my thoughts become unusually heavy. As I raised my right hand to my eyes, I saw that my fingers started to evaporate. This time, they didn't dissolve in smoke, but transformed into strange, small multicolored bubbles. "Oh… It's starting," I said while looking at the woman sitting to my right. After watching my hands for a few moments and being overcome with excessive fatigue, I collapsed on my mat. I must have lost consciousness almost instantly because I could not remember having had any visions when I came back to my senses.

When I reopened my eyes, I felt heavy and nauseous. Looking around me, the setting was dark and gloomy. It was cold. Completely lost in this unexpected environment, I tried to look for comfort in the look of my friends nearby, but I realized with dismay that the vast majority of them were slumped on the ground, seemingly lifeless, their faces pale and white. Some people were vomiting outside of the circle, making grotesque noises. The air was incredibly heavy. When my eyelids closed under the intense fatigue, nightmarish visions flashed through my head. Amongst them, I saw satanic smiles, dirty teeth close-ups, pieces of putrid meat, and swarms of worms, as well as an endless succession of tunnels and a multitude of impressive images follow each other in slow motion. I could not believe that I was in such a nightmare. Nothing had prepared me for that. I tried to mentally replace the visions with beautiful colored shapes, like I did several times the night before, but to no avail. When one tunnel closed, another one opened immediately after, relentlessly. Panic-stricken, I opened my eyes and sat up straight. After spending a long time lost in an indescribable stupor, I slowly regained my senses. The horrible visions faded away. With great effort and my entire body shaking, I put on a jacket that I took the precaution of bringing along before the ceremony per the advice of a caring friend.

The sight around me was macabre. The glow of the full moon dramatically emphasized the outlines of the dense jungle that was just a few steps away. The giant silhouettes of the saw-toothed palm leaves, high and menacing, appeared ready to attack.

There was something incredibly ominous in the air. I then realized that the shamans had started chanting. At the top of their lungs, they shouted monotonous syllables over and over, with a power and intensity that I had never heard before. I was completely hypnotized. Each cry pounded my mind like a sledgehammer. My thoughts seemed imprisoned by the unrelenting incantations. Due to the extreme fatigue, I needed all my mental strength to keep my eyes open because as soon as they closed, the nightmarish visions violently reappeared. And above all, I was feeling increasingly nauseous.

"Why is there no music? Why these horrible chants?" I thought, "How can I escape this?" I added while staring at the empty sky.

Since the ceremony the night before, I was acutely aware of the influence that sound had on the shamanic experience of ayahuasca. I then came to the conclusion that harmonious music would help me escape the torpor and crippling hypnosis that I was trapped in. "Why is the music taking so long to come?" I lamented while looking at the immobile and Machiavellian Moon in the lifeless sky. I relentlessly tried to fight the nightmarish visions, and every time I succeeded in opening my eyes, I turned to the shamans to mentally beg them to stop the incantations and start the music.

After what seemed like an eternity, I was completely exhausted. I could not think clearly anymore. My eyelids were extremely heavy. I only had one objective, which was not to give in to the nightmarish visions. I was terrified by the idea that they could take me down to a hell-like realm and invade my soul. I was convinced that I was going to yield at some point if I remained seated any longer.

At that moment, I could only see one practical way to escape the mental torture, to save my soul: music. "I need music. If I put my hand on my mobile phone, I can surely end this hell." I made extraordinary efforts to stand up. Pale and powerless, my back arched and my head still down, I took a few steps outside of the shamanic circle while trying to hide my horror as best I could. I felt terribly intoxicated. Barefoot, shaking and dragging one foot in front of the other, I walked towards my hut which was about three hundred feet away. On the path, I came across some villagers wearing their imposing feather headdresses. As it was very dark, I only saw their gloomy and frightening silhouettes. The feathers of their headdresses looked like long and sharpened blades. With my head down, I pretended not to look at them for fear that they would stop me or order me to go back to the infernal circle. At that point, I was convinced that the ceremony was satanic. I had become paranoid.

As soon as I reached my hut, I grabbed my flashlight that was on the windowsill next to my tent and turned it on to find my phone. After a few minutes, I instinctively raised my head towards the entrance of the hut which was about three meters away from me. As I saw the silhouette of a man wearing a large headdress sitting on the doorstep, my heart skipped a beat. The villager seemed to be watching me. "Oh gosh… He knows I am here. He's going to call the others to come and take me by force." Seized with panic, I turned my flashlight off and swiftly slipped into my tent. As soon as I closed my eyes, the nightmarish visions reappeared. A few minutes later, unable to stay confined in the closed space of the small tent, I quietly opened the zip just enough to let my head out. The man wearing the headdress had left. Relieved, I exited the tent to keep searching for my mobile phone, but this time, without my flashlight.

After looking in one of my bags on the floor in vain, I remembered that at the canteen, I had asked Yogesh to put my phone in the hut before I went for a shower. I looked in Yogesh and Aesha's bags near the tent, but I did not find anything. I felt nauseous again. In desperation, I summoned my guardian spirits to help me: "If you are real, please do something…" With a desperately foggy mind, I walked in circles in the hut, lamenting my fate: "Why did I decide to come here? If I make it out alive, I will never, ever, take part in such ceremonies again!" I declared, staring at the roof of the hut. "That's enough! I need to come back to my senses. I have to find the phone!" I added. Still in the dark, I grabbed another bag laid against the wall that separated the two rooms. While searching it, I was terrified by the idea of coming into contact with the repugnant objects of my visions. Still no phone.

Shortly after, I walked towards the door, stopped for a few moments, walked down the three steps, moved in large circles in front of the hut, cursed at my plight while looking up at the sky, then stopped suddenly and exclaimed: "Try again. I need music!" Back in the hut, I searched every bag that was within reach. Nothing.

Then, two meters away from my friends' tent, on the windowsill, I saw a small bag in which they placed items that they used frequently. It was a backpack with a small pouch at the front. "This is it!" I murmured with glee. After opening the zip and putting my hand in the small pouch, I felt a phone-shaped object. I quickly took it out of its case and realized that it was indeed mine. "I am saved." After pressing the power button for a few seconds, nothing appeared on the screen. The battery was flat. "I have a portable charger!" Still feeling intoxicated but happy to have a solution in sight, I searched my bags one after the other until I found what I was looking for. Shortly after plugging my phone into the charger, the battery charge indicator lit up. "Where did I put my headphones? How is it that I have managed to scatter everything like this!" I said to myself, laughing on the inside. I eventually put my hands on them after a few minutes. My phone was finally giving signs of life.

During the boat trip on the way to the village, I had inadvertently jumped into the river with my phone in my trouser pocket. I knew that if I turned it on immediately after getting out of the water, it would short-circuit and probably be irreversibly out of order. To make sure that it dried completely before turning it back on, and per the advice of my friends, I put it in a small bowl full of rice grains which was meant to absorb the humidity of the device. The day before this ceremony, when I powered it on, the screen flashed several times before switching itself off again. Now, over twenty-four hours later, I did not know whether it was going to power on. It was the moment of truth. "If the gods are with me, there is no way that this can't work." After pressing the main switch for a few seconds, the screen lit up. With shaking hands and excitement, I hit the music application icon and pressed play. Soft music crawled into my ears. "Finally!" Even though I was still nauseous and scared that the villagers would see me, I felt extremely happy at the thought of being saved.

I immediately felt better. "I was right, sound is paramount in the shamanic experience." Convinced that I was finally going to rest, I lay on the floor. However, as soon as I closed my eyes, the violent and nightmarish visions reappeared. To my dismay, I realized that the power of the shamanic incantations went through my headphones. "If music doesn't help me, I'm lost..." The nausea became uncontrollable. I ran to the rail of the hut to vomit, but to no avail.

I exited the hut with my headphones still in my ears and walked on the sand, making repetitive large circles on the outskirts of the hut. I went back inside and lay in my hammock, then in the tent, and finally on the floor. Nothing was working. I went back out and stared at the sky, asking what I could possibly have done to deserve to be in this situation, to be in such agony. I prayed to the gods, to my guardian angels, to the spirits of nature, and to the divine spirits to come to my rescue, but to no avail. I looked for the light at the end of the long tunnel, for an eternity, but I did not find it. I came to the conclusion that shamanism, or at least this particular type of shamanism, was satanic. It was inconceivable to me that honest and sincere participants had to go through such a nightmare to grow spiritually.

When I reentered into the hut, powerless and crippled by fatigue, I leaned on the rail. While mechanically turning my attention to the shamanic circle, I noticed the silhouettes of the participants gathered around the fire. Suddenly, from out of nowhere, a voice whispered in my ear: "Go and save the others. Save them from the satanic grip." I was aghast. After wandering a few moments in a state of total confusion, I exclaimed: "This is probably the same voice that the great religious men once heard. They were also asked to save the masses…" In less than an instant, a plan of Divine Rescue had formed before my eyes. "*This* is a challenge that I must successfully overcome, just like those that were given to the great religious people!"

I then remembered that one of the participants, Joseph, had used portable speakers to accompany the projection of photographs for the children of the village. To the sound of peaceful music, they sat in front of the screen for hours watching the photographs taken by Joseph. I needed to find my friend so he could tell me where he placed his speakers. "But how will he act if he, like the other participants around the fire, is under the satanic hold?" My plan of action was to put the speakers in the center of the maloca, plug them into my phone, and gather all of the participants to get them away from the hypnotic incantations. "That way, they will be saved." It was a relatively simple plan to become a great hero, I believed.

After few minutes lost in my thoughts, I came back to my senses, "I cannot do something so foolish! It makes no sense. My ego is surely playing tricks on me." I felt nauseous again. I tried to vomit several times, but nothing was working. Then, I heard the voice again: "Save the others." Strangely, I felt nauseous every time I ignored the 'Order from Above.' The more times it was repeated to me, the more I was convinced by its truth. "I need to save the others. This mission will make me a hero. This is very probably why I am here and why this ceremony is taking place right now. It is surely to test my strength and willpower," I solemnly declared.

I left the hut and walked towards the shamanic circle. When I arrived to the outskirts, my headphones still in my ears, I watched my friends for a few moments. However, at that short distance from the shamans, the music coming from my headphones was not loud enough to mitigate the satanic chants. Not only was I unable to think clearly, but the nightmarish visions, even though less aggressive with my eyes open, reappeared.

While looking at the participants in front of me around the circle, I saw Yogesh. He was lying down on the ground in the fetal position, his face in the sand. Bernard was sitting next to him. I smiled at Bernard. When he returned a smiled, the expression of his unusually wide eyes shocked me. "Oh no… He is under the satanic influence. I shouldn't look at him for too long." I immediately turned to Yogesh. With great difficulty, I crouched, grabbed his unusually heavy and lifeless hand, and pulled it slowly towards me to get my friend into a seated position. His complexion was pale and his expression lifeless. "It's too late," I sadly told myself. With a calm voice, I slowly articulated: "Yogesh… Get up, brother. Yogesh. Yogesh. You need to sit down, my friend. You need to regain consciousness. You cannot remain lying down. It's not good for you." Yogesh slowly opened his eyes. His gaze was empty, like a drunkard possessed by alcohol. I thought that I had seen a smile of gratitude, but I was not sure as it was too dark. I raised my thumb and told him: "It will be fine, brother, it will be fine. Hang in there. Be brave." He was apparently still smiling, which gave me confidence in what I was doing. "Yogesh is now saved," I concluded, letting go of his hand while standing up.

I took a few steps to try and do the same thing with the others, but as I mechanically turned around, I saw Bernard rushing towards Yogesh, then gently and repetitively tapping Yogesh's back, breathing tobacco smoke on his body, from his feet to his head, then fanned his face with a long and large feather. I was petrified. "Oh gosh… What have I done? I shouldn't have disturbed Yogesh!" I had realized that I had just broken one of the fundamental rules of ayahuasca ceremonies: never disturb a participant, under *any* circumstances, unless they call for help or is in clear and imminent danger. The thought of acting as a savior became absolute heresy. "What is this sordid voice? I don't understand… Is it really my ego?" I took a few steps back. "Have I just made the most absurd mistake that could ever be made?" I repeated ad infinitum. I took a few steps outside of the circle and saw a woman sitting on a small wooden bench. I walked towards her with a smile and sat at her side. She looked surprisingly expressionless. I glanced at her for an instant, hoping that she would show me a sign of gratitude for my heroic act, but she remained expressionless the whole time. More lost than ever, I stood back up and took a few steps along the circle. I came across another participant. We greeted each other with a nod, then I saw that he was speaking to me. As I still had my headphones in my ears, I did not understand what he was saying. I was too confused and lost to take them out. However, based on his gestures, I understood that he had vomited a lot during the ceremony. "How lucky!" I exclaimed in my mind, "He regurgitated the evil inside of him. I would have loved for that to happen to me as well."

A few steps away, I saw Joseph, the owner of the much sought-after speakers. "Is it still worth it? Have I not let this insane idea already go?——No, it's surely a sign from above to meet him here and now, when I am about to give up. I need to keep going." Forgetting that I still had my headphones in my ears, I said to him: "You have speakers to play music outdoors, right?" Looking surprised, he nodded. I quickly took out one of my headphones and let it hang to my neck. "Are they in your hut?" He nodded again, but this time, he seemed annoyed. Unlike me, Joseph appeared comfortable in his skin, in no way disturbed by the satanic chants. "Hmm … he must be one of them…" I concluded. I wanted us to fetch the tool I needed to accomplish my mission, but how could I make him understand that? He swiftly turned his head towards the headphone that was still in my right ear. "Oh no, he's seen the headphone," I told myself, taking half a step back. He pointed his index finger at my ear. "Oh, that… I need music. Why is there no music yet? It is vital to me," I answered unconvincingly, looking towards the shamans. At this point, I couldn't muster up the courage to share my plan of rescue with him. Joseph, looking exasperated, turned around and walked quickly towards the shamans. "What if I have just made a monumental mistake? And, why do most of the participants seem at ease with the shamanic chants even though there is no music? Am I the only one who feels horrified?" A thousand questions were going through my mind. I was paralyzed and submerged by the panic. "I cannot have been *that* wrong. No way… No way, not *me*…" I mentally kept telling myself, feverishly looking at the sky to find a sign of support, as small as it could have been. But I saw no sign. I felt a nervous tremor going through my entire body. I felt completely lost. I wanted to escape this place. Knowing now that it had all been a foolish mistake, I mentally implored the sky for a strong wind to take me far away from here. But no wind blew that night.

"There is no point taking the participants to the hut, near the speakers. No one cares! Besides, those who are looking at me are surely wondering what I'm doing here, standing alone with my headphones on." I saw Bernard, walking towards the maloca. I moved towards him and tapped his shoulder. He continued to move forward without looking at me. "He knows what I have done..." I lowered my head. A thousand questions made me feel a thousand regrets. Jesus the Savior... The diabolical chants... The state of hypnosis... Panic... Every action that I had taken was playing before my eyes like the choppy scenes of a Hitchcock movie.

Suddenly and, most unexpectedly, the incantations stopped. A few minutes later, accompanied by drum rolls and guitars, the shamans began to sing. The music that I had been hoping for had just arrived. In the space of a few moments, the heavy and ominous atmosphere was swept away to give way to a light and almost enchanted landscape. Some villagers crossed the circle to form the 'snake dance'. Almost mechanically, a handful of participants stood up to follow them. Others straightened up and slowly removed the fine sand from their faces, hair, and clothes. Others, still lying down, stretched their limbs. Some packed up their belongings and made their way to their huts. There was no more doubt. I had done the most ridiculous thing that could be done during ayahuasca ceremonies. "So, the shamans... These ceremonies... They are not satanic. I imagined *all of that*..." I replayed backwards everything that happened during the evening: Joseph, the speakers, Bernard, Yogesh, the 'Voice from Above', the mental torture, the man wearing the large feather headdress who watched me from the doorstep, the silhouettes of the villagers, the nightmarish visions... I replayed the film again, and again. "Oh gosh... How am I going to overcome this now? How embarrassing... How am I going to face my friends tomorrow morning? Their senses are so keen that they will read me like an open book." I took a few steps back and looked around me, then lay down on the sand. I was so desperate that I did not have the courage to look at anyone. I was convinced beyond a shadow of a doubt that I had imagined everything. "Maybe I should have given in to the visions. They surely would have destroyed my *ego*, which *is* what caused all of these incredible events," I thought while staring at the disappearing stars.

I remained lost in my countless thoughts for a long while, then stood up to go to the hut. I saw Yogesh in front of the canteen. "Yogesh, my friend, how are you? I'm so sorry to have disturbed you..." I told him with a voice filled with regret. I knew I had interrupted something that I should not have when I woke him up. I almost wanted him to get angry, but Yogesh remained calm. He smiled at me and said, "No, Adriano, you did the right thing. I think you came at the right time. I needed that, and when I looked at you, you smiled at me, so I trusted you."

Even though my friend's words were relieving, they were not enough to reassure me. I was convinced that I had interrupted a process that could have benefited my friend's spiritual growth.

I returned to my hut, then collapsed on the floor of the tent, full of regret.

That morning, it took me a long time to find sleep.

❄ ❄ ❄

As soon as I woke up, I endeavored to find the people whom I interacted with the night before. Yogesh reassured me once again; he probably understood what really happened and forgave me. Bernard reprimanded me softly by explaining the potential dangers of what I did, which he said was irresponsible; he was right. For obvious reasons, I neglected to tell him that a 'Voice from Above' had ordered me to do what I did. Joseph, the owner of the speakers, asked me why I was looking for music during the ceremony. He then reprimanded me for trying to change the course of a ceremony, "The music begins when it has to," he said in a dry tone.

Three flute sounds signaled lunch. I was dreading this moment, but I knew I would have to face the other participants sooner or later. "If I meet Scott, Asil, or Rory, one of the three pillars of the shamanic ceremonies, I could ask them questions about what happened to me. But, how can I possibly explain that I tried to incarnate the 'Savior of Humanity'?"

On the way to the canteen, the same question from the night before came back to me: "What if, instead of fighting, I had given in fully to the events of the ceremony, even to the dark visions? What would I be like today? Would I be a better person?——" "Most probably," I added.

I was fortunate enough to meet Scott on the path, on the outskirts of the canteen. Scott is Australian. He is in his forties and has lived in London for many years. He seems very nice and has quite a lot of experience with ayahuasca ceremonies. He has followed a spiritual path since his childhood. For many years, he was a businessman and making a very good living. After a few bad experiences in the business world, he left his job to dive full-time into a spiritual journey. Based on what I have heard from his close friends, he is now providing spiritual training that is very successful.

When I met Scott, I asked him if we could walk a bit further to talk. I did not want the other participants to hear us. He nodded. We sat on a bench on the outskirts of the canteen. It was not far enough for me, but I sat down anyway; I *had* to talk to someone. Scott listened to me very carefully as I recounted what had happened the night before. Except for the part when I tried to incarnate the 'Savior of Humanity', I told him everything in great detail: the nightmarish images, hell, the battle at night where I did not close my eyes at all, and the music that I thought was satanic.

"Why all of this?" I asked in total dismay, staring at the ground. "Is there a connection between the chants, which *I* consider to be satanic, and what I experienced?" Surely out of courtesy, Scott did not answer immediately. I was not surprised, because I knew that my experience was entirely made up by my intrepid imagination and ruthless ego. After listening to me carefully, he looked in my eyes and told me that what happened—the events I recounted—was not that important. According to him, the aim of this type of ceremony is to give the participants the opportunity to become stronger spiritually and not to succumb to darkness.

"Scott, so that means I succeeded since I didn't succumb to the nightmarish visions?" As soon as I finished asking that question, I realized how futile it was.

"Hmm … You have to be strong, but you shouldn't have to fight," he added while smiling politely. "You see, you need to be able to keep the light, even in the most trying situations. That is the goal."

His advice made sense to me.

Scott added that last night's ceremony was particularly difficult because it took place during a supermoon.

"It was a 'cura'[1] ceremony!" he exclaimed, laughing nervously. "The aim of such healing ceremony is to give the participants the opportunity to do deep work on themselves in order to heal and surpass their spiritual limits," he added.

My friend reassured me that last night was not only difficult for all of us, but for the shamans as well.

Scott's attention and explanations were extremely calming to me. Even if they unequivocally confirmed that I was wrong to act the way that I did, I had fresh hope. I would need to adapt my behavior to this new knowledge during the next ceremony.

"Thank you, Scott, for your precious advice. I'll do better next time," I said, smiling and tapping him on the shoulder.

❄ ❄ ❄

In the afternoon, a group of Russian cameramen arrived in the village to film a documentary on the Huni Kuin people, shamanism, and ayahuasca. This news cast a chill within our group. Most participants were worried that the group harmony that we had

1. 'Cura' means 'cure,' in the sense of 'healing ceremony.'

would irreversibly be disturbed. Certain participants were angry—
and probably felt that it was unfair—that the team of cameramen
arrived here on a helicopter, whereas we had to travel by boat along
the never-ending and winding river for five days. Others were com-
plaining about losing their intimacy and anonymity, which they
considered to be particularly important for their spiritual development. Just before coming to the Amazon I took the time to watch
two documentaries about ayahuasca, and both of them showed the
same sordid scenes: a group of people with psychological issues
taking part in ayahuasca ceremonies, and because most scenes were
filmed using infrared video cameras, the participants appeared as
possessed beings, rolling on the ground, eyes open wide, screaming
and vomiting uncontrollably. It was obvious that no sane person
would want to appear on such a program.

That afternoon, just like after each ceremony, we sat down in a
circle around sacred ritual objects, flowers, tea leaves, and fresh
fruits, to share our experiences. During that session, the group of
Russian cameramen joined us. They had heard of our complaints
and probably wanted to clear the air as soon as possible. The discussion turned out to be quite tense. Both sides would need to nego-
tiate and make concessions for the village to be harmonious once
more. At the end of the endless discussions, it was decided that a
small and private ceremony would be organized towards the last
days of the festival for the purpose of the documentary.

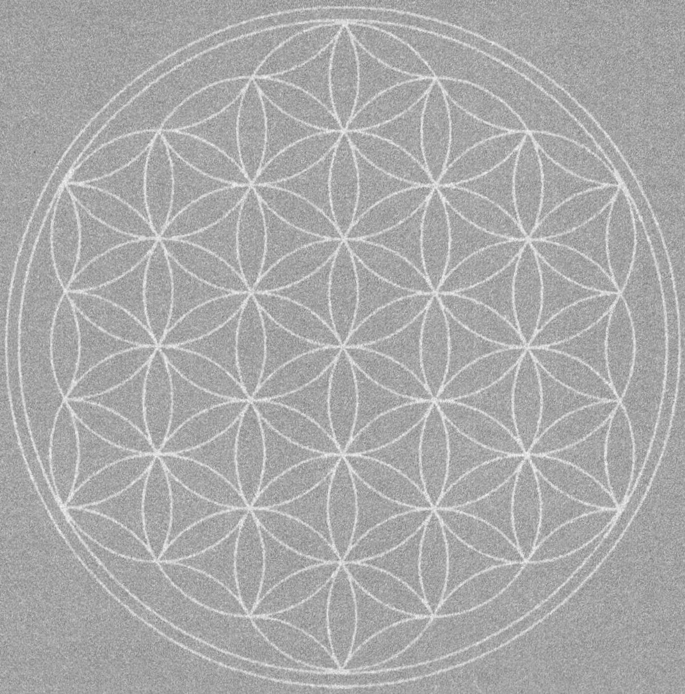

Third Ceremony
An Unexpected Near-Death Experience

Death, my son, is a good thing for all men;
it is the night for this worried day that we call life.
—Jacques Henri Bernardin de Saint-Pierre

November 16, 2016

As evening approached, I decided to seek help from my friends to avoid repeating the same mistakes during the upcoming ceremony. I was walking towards the maloca when I saw Rory on the outskirts of the canteen. He seemed to be going in the same direction.

Rory is an Englishman in his forties. He is naturally quiet, speaks very little and chooses his words carefully. It seems to me that few people truly know him. He surrounds himself almost exclusively with close friends, like Scott, Asil, and a few other rare souls who are fortunate enough to gain his true friendship. That said, because of his pleasant nature, he easily gets along with everyone. Rory has a relationship with minerals that I can only describe as extraordinary due to the fact that he uses them to heal all sorts of ailments. He also seems to perceive and interact with higher dimensions of his surroundings through waves or vibrations. His broad knowledge of subjects related to shamanism and spirituality left me curious and intrigued more than once.

After sharing my worries about how I should behave during the coming ceremony, Rory paused for a moment, then told me in a calm and reassuring voice:

"I completely understand your concern, Adriano. These questions are asked frequently, especially at the beginning."

He paused again, then added:

"This is what I think. First of all, it is important not to lie down, but to stay seated for as long as possible while keeping your spine straight, in the Earth-sky axis. Otherwise, it is almost impossible not to succumb to the visions or fall asleep."

He looked at the sky for a few moments and continued:

"Next, do not lose yourself in your thoughts. Give in to the present moment. This is achievable if you stay focused on your breathing. By following your breath, the mind, which is very often responsible for all our woes, loses its grip, thereby opening the door to the spirit world."

Just like Scott and Asil, Rory often gave me precious advice that proved to be extremely useful in difficult times while under the influence of ayahuasca.

This ceremony, like the following ones, was to take place outdoors, in the same location as the night before. I dreaded this choice.

Just before the three flute sounds marked the fateful hour, I asked Scott, Asil, and Rory if I could sit next to them to seek their help and protection if needed. I was not really surprised to learn, however, that I was neither the only nor the first person to have had the same idea. Apparently, the seats had been reserved long in advance. I resigned myself to find another spot as near as possible to them, which was six or seven participants away. I sat between Hernan, the Argentine, and Veronica, the young British woman.

The shamans, donning long and white ceremonial robes adorned with colored geometrical patterns and wearing impressive headdresses, finally arrived. They sat to our right, a few meters away from Hernan, Veronica and me. As per usual, the jar containing the ayahuasca was standing on the small wooden table, just in front of Ninawa. At the sight of it, a shiver ran up my spine; it reminded me of the tragic events that took place the night before.

After hesitating for some time, I joined the long queue to receive the ayahuasca. As I approached Ninawa, I watched him to see if he smiled at the other participants before me while holding the potion out to them. He did not. He kept his serious and solemn gaze. When my turn came, he smiled. His expression seemed even more disturbing than the night before. Was he trying to say that ayahuasca was not for me? Was the impressive shaman quietly uttering: "Hmm, don't you understand? Do you still not comprehend the signs?" Was it actually happening or was I dreaming? I was confused.

To the intention I stated during the previous ceremonies, I added the wish to improve my behavior in the face of the dark visions should they appear again and truly be necessary to my spiritual development.

The ayahuasca had the same awful taste as the one served the night before. Once the bitter concoction swallowed, I sat on my mat. Even though I almost immediately felt a nearly irresistible urge to vomit, I was able to control it by focusing my thoughts on the movements of my breath. I felt the first effects of ayahuasca after about twenty minutes. I must have lost consciousness shortly after because the only memories that I now have are those of the nightmarish visions and hypnotic sensations that followed. Before my horrified eyes, in addition to the disturbing images from the night before, knife-like shapes wearing vivid colors were making swift and precise movements across the entire sky. I quickly realized that the powerful incantations were orchestrating the gloomy march. The power transmitted by the chants were far beyond anything I had ever experienced. The incantations resonated as if we were in an immense and eerie abandoned cathedral. It was inconceivable that such immense power and mindless violence could come from conventional human beings. Each monotonous syllable that these mechanical robots yelled ad infinitum prevented me from collecting my thoughts.

The chants continued relentlessly, for an interminably long time, during which I tried with all my strength to resist, to fight, not to succumb to the intoxicating hypnosis, but my strength was diminishing far too quickly. At that point, all I could think of was to collapse to the ground, pass out, and forget everything that had ever happened. "How much longer is this going to last?" I yelled silently while imploring the sky, draining the ounce of energy that I had left.

After fighting forces that were clearly far greater than mine, I finally gave up. There was clearly no point to continue. "My foolishness and credulity have led me here again," I thought, "how could I have been so naive?" I now needed to escape this desperate situation at all costs. This time, I did not have any shame about doing the same thing as I did the night before if it could save me from this nightmare. I was convinced that I had to escape. It was a life-and-death situation. My goal was clear: making it out this ceremony alive, no matter how. The only way that I knew was music. Even though it had not proven itself to be very effective during the previous ceremony, it was my only known ally.

Strangely, all the precious pieces of advice given by Scott, Rory and Asil did not even cross my mind.

Lost in my confused thoughts for a long moment, weary and exhausted, I finally gathered enough strength to stand up and walk towards my hut. I exactly knew the path and how to behave in order to not arouse suspicion when I left the circle and came across the villagers on my way to the hut. I simply had to execute the same steps as I did the day before, in the exact same sequence.

Before the ceremony started, I took the precaution of placing my mobile phone and headphones in a visible spot, on the shelf next to my tent. Arrived at my hut, I grabbed my phone and put my headphones in my ears, then started the music. To my dismay, not only did it not weaken the power of the visions, which I had feared, it made me nervous. The shamanic chants added to the music were hammering my mind even further. All of the symptoms from the night before reappeared: insurmountable fatigue, nausea, and a total inability to organize my thoughts. However, contrary to the night before, I refrained from incarnating the 'Savior of Humanity,' which made me smile.

Convinced that I was going to succumb to an irreversible madness if I stayed for a moment longer under the hypnotic effect of the chants, in turn, I sat on the doorstep, lay down in my tent, across the wooden floor, in my hammock, and walked in hundreds of circles in the sand outside the hut. I thought that by doing so, the sun would eventually rise and all would be over. But the time was too long. Far too long. The incantations were gaining more and more ground. When I opened my eyes, a thousand questions and regrets entered my exhausted mind. When I closed them, the nightmarish visions reappeared, relentlessly.

I condemned the sky and swore at the gods. I cursed myself even more. "None of this is you, Adriano. You like the light, so why are you taking part in these satanic rituals? A spiritual path should *not* go this way," I shouted at myself over and over while looking at the sky, hoping for an answer. But silence was all I could hear. "Don't You see?" I said while addressing the empty sky, "Don't You see that every step I have taken since childhood has been to get closer to You, to elevate myself?" But there was no way out. I was trapped in my own fate, exhausted and clearly condemned by the gods for having the audacity to play with the Fire of Darkness. "This will teach you not to make the same mistake in your next life," they probably yelled, perched on their celestial thrones, pointing at me, tired of adding another being amongst the countless fallen souls.

After what seemed like an eternity, I felt the urge to vomit again. The thought of regurgitating the brew responsible for my agony suddenly restored hope.

When I was in India to practice yoga, we had to force ourselves every early morning to vomit the two liters of lukewarm salt water we had just quickly gulped down. It was an excellent exercise to purify the body that proved to be very effective against fatigue and excess acidity.

Facing outside and leaning against the hut rail, I took a bottle of water that was next to the hammock and drank its content without taking a breath. As soon as I dropped the bottle on the ground, I pushed my fingers down my throat to vomit. After a few tries, a very acidic liquid emerged from my entrails. Even if I felt lighter and fresher, the effects of the incantations reappeared after a few moments, pounding my mind. I could see the dark visions again as soon as I closed my eyes. I made myself vomit several more times, but the result was invariably the same.

❄ ❄ ❄

It was now late in the night. I had been tirelessly looking for strength deep into my soul, in places that I did not know existed. I had probably reached the limits of human resistance. The idea of fighting the hold of the hypnotic chants, the nightmarish visions, and the weariness had become somewhat absurd. Looking at the ground beneath my feet, all I could think of was to lie down, close my eyes, and forget that I had ever walked this Earth. Surrendering had become an inevitable end. I somehow knew that I was about to die.

Under the weight of a deep sadness and solitude, my legs slowly bent until my knees touched the floor. Head down, and probably out of self-respect, I wanted to accomplish one final thing before life left my body: the idea that my beloved friends would find me inanimate in the middle of the hut, on the wooden floor, was unbearable. I needed to leave with at least a shred of dignity.

With great strength and patience, I slowly bent my body forward and put my right hand flat on the floor. Once I had found the right balance, I lifted my left knee with the help of my other hand and slid my foot until it was flat on the ground. With both hands on the floor, I now had enough balance to do the same with my right knee. I then could stand up with both feet flat on the ground. With my head down, back arched, and legs slightly bent, I started to move towards the tent. I was thoroughly exhausted, but I had to succeed. Each movement and thought were draining my energy. I needed to breathe deeply between each step, between each thought. Once I reached the entrance of the tent, I crouched very carefully in order not to lose balance, then slid my hand along the zipper. I had to do it several times to find the loop, which was at the bottom, near the ground. With the help of my thumb and index finger, I grabbed it and pulled it upwards. Once the zipper was open enough, I let my entire body collapse on the floor of the tent. I had to wriggle several times to be able to lie flat on my back with my legs straight and my arms down my body. While in that position, with my head on the deflated pillow, I noticed a glow that infiltrated through the opening of the tent. The idea of closing it properly crossed my mind but I let the thought evaporate. I felt my eyelids close, then it became all dark.

"What a wonderful feeling to finally give in. Why do we fear death so much after all?" I murmured silently. Finally, a moment of respite. Surprisingly, there were no more mechanical robots screaming infernal and repetitive syllables. No more nightmarish visions scrolling in front of my eyes either. I had nowhere to go. I had nowhere to be. I had no more desires. My world had become utterly quiet and peaceful. I knew that everything was as it should be, like the perfection that is unattainable in our physical reality. I had no more regrets either. No more plans for the future. For what was probably the first time in my life, I gave in to the moment. "Our last moments are so peaceful," I remarked. I felt that a just few final heartbeats and deep and long breaths were still keeping me in my body, and each of them seemed to last an eternity. "What a gentle symphony," I thought. "Why have I never listened to it until now?"

I was in peace. I was happy. I was ready.

After a few moments absorbed in the hollow sound of my heavy heartbeat and faint breath, an intense light filled the entire horizon. It was such a peculiar feeling that I sensed the light had come from very far. The next moment, I was lying on an immense and abnormally bright green lawn. The vast sky was filled with a light of an intensity that is unseen of in our physical dimensions. The azure ceiling scrolled at a breathtaking speed, like a stroboscope describing the acceleration of time. Then, a symphony of a hundred thousand instruments occupied the space. They resonated as if I was in an immense cathedral. Each of the music notes generated electric shocks at an almost intolerable intensity that went through my spine in violent fits and starts. They seemed to be coming from my legs in torrential waves and at a constantly growing intensity. Sharp pains and intense pleasure alternated for a very long time. I then felt my body becoming increasingly heavier, my head tipping to the left, my teeth becoming loose and dropping, my jaw decomposing, my hands, arms, legs, organs, and finally my skeleton, turning into dust, all at the pulsating beat of the stroboscope.

I knew that, on the physical plane, I was not alive anymore. I sensed that I was in a vast and infinite space, between worlds. I felt deep ecstasy. I then saw my chakras[1] light up one by one like a giant firework filling the sky. Holding a dagger of light in his hands and showing infinite compassion in his eyes, a being of light approached me. I felt he was prepared to dive it into my heart. I do not know what happened after that because I lost consciousness as he approached me further.

※ ※ ※

When I recovered my senses, I had the strange feeling that I had regained control of the fingertips on my left hand, then, a few moments later, of those on my right hand. Like a child who discovered his limbs for the first time and is surprised by the new sensation, I moved my fingers in a repetitive back-and-forth motion. Then, I felt as if my other hand, my arms, and the other parts of my body were recomposing one after the other. Still in ecstasy, I became aware that I was reintegrating my physical body.

A voice, surely from the depths of my soul, addressed me: "You now have a choice. You can either leave the world that you belong to and join us by continuing to bathe in this ecstasy, or stay and work with your peers." Even though I was amazed by the message

---

1. Chakras are the various focal points in the subtle body used in a variety of ancient meditation practices, collectively denominated as Tantra, or the esoteric or inner traditions of Indian religion, Chinese Taoism, Tibetan Buddhism, as well as Japanese Esoteric Buddhism, and in postmodernity, in new age medicine, and originally psychologically adopted to the western mind through the assistance of Carl G. Jung. — Source: Wikipedia.

as well as the gentleness and unusual depth of the voice, I did not hesitate for longer than a short moment. My decision was final: I would stay here, on Earth. "Then get up, now," the voice continued. Exceedingly surprised by the ease with which I had just regained control of my body, I sat up in one continuous and swift movement. Still feeling ecstatic, I opened the tent with a steady hand, walked the few meters that separated me from the doorstep, and left the hut with graceful ease. I could not wait to rejoin the shamanic circle where my friends were. "But this time, not as the 'Savior of the World'!" I told myself while laughing.

It was now dawn. To my pleasant surprise, the incantations had stopped to finally make way to the music that I had waited for so long. "The shamans must have become human again!" I thought, smilingly. As is it the custom after the chants, a few villagers wearing headdresses, bright paintings and ornaments were singing in harmony with the shamans while performing the snake dance around the fire. That morning, the melody was even more beautiful and exquisite than during the previous ceremonies. Without hesitating, I joined the dancers. While dancing to the rhythm of the music, I was in a state of bliss. The sensation of the silky sand under my feet gave me so much joy that I felt I was barely touching the ground. I had the impression that I could have brushed the sky with my hand if I had dared to. The voice which had now become familiar told me: "You can recreate what you are feeling now at any moment if you wish to."

I looked around me and noticed that some of my friends had had a difficult night. Even if it hurt to think about what they had probably gone through, I knew that everything would eventually be fine, that they were protected, that benevolent and charitable spirits were by their side no matter what.

Even though I wished to remain in this state of ecstasy for the rest of my life, I knew that I would inevitably have to return to the harsh reality of day-to-day life in the very near future. However, I thought that it did not matter to me because having had that experience just once would be enough for eternity. I had no more doubt. I was here and present.

Hernan was also dancing. I liked him a lot because he was the kind of person who remained positive no matter what happened. In a very short time, he had become the mascot of the group. I passed by the few dancers that separated us to get to him. I tapped his shoulder, we shared a smile and hugged.

"Are you okay brother?" I asked him.

"Yes, brother, I am well," he exclaimed with a big smile. He did indeed look radiant.

I continued to take part in the snake dance for an hour more, then sat next to Hernan. Veronica was lying on the ground in the fetal position. She was slowly wriggling with her hands on her stomach. She apparently had had a difficult night. One of her friends was by her side. I put my hand on Veronica's head in order to soothe her. After a few minutes, the expression on her face did not improve, so I removed my hand. After exchanging a few words with Hernan, I looked at Veronica again to see if her condition had improved. Asil, one the veterans of ayahuasca ceremonies, was by her side. He had a crystal ball in his right hand that he was holding a few inches above Veronica's stomach. He seemed to be uttering words, perhaps incantations. This was extraordinary to me, but after everything that I had experienced in these ceremonies, I thought that not a lot could surprise me anymore. I turned my attention to Hernan who began to speak to me again.

After about ten minutes, while mechanically glancing towards the fire, I saw Veronica. She was sitting next to the fire, immobile, her arms holding her knees. She was staring at the fire, absorbed in her thoughts, looking calm and serene. "What did Asil do for Veronica to recover that quickly? Did he extract a malevolent entity from her body with the help of the crystal ball? It is a mystery that I will have to explore." I thought, amazed. "There are so many things that we cannot understand. Why is this not taught to us?" I mused.

Sitting down with my elbows on my knees, my head between my hands, and my eyes closed, an intense light suddenly appeared before me. The voice inside me spoke again: "Knowledge. You are going to acquire more knowledge." Without thinking and with my eyes still shut, I immediately replied: "Yes… I want to learn more, but not without wisdom and compassion." I knew that acquiring knowledge without those two essential components was dangerous. History is filled with tragic examples. A sphere divided into three equal parts, labelled 'KNOWLEDGE,' 'WISDOM,' and 'COMPASSION' appeared at the middle of the vast light. While the sphere grew larger, I was under the impression that it was recharging my brain with a blue, luminescent energy.

"Hey, brother, are you okay?"

It was Hernan, tapping my shoulder. He must have been worried seeing me sitting still with my head down between my hands. I immediately thought that the recharging process was going to stop. However, I was not disappointed. I intuitively knew that I had acquired the knowledge I was meant to receive. I smiled at Hernan. We spoke a few minutes before he went to sleep.

I closed my eyes again. I felt that the voice was still inside me. I addressed it to ask for better health, more energy, and more vitality. I also told it that I wanted to understand why we were here, on Earth, and why there were so many incomprehensible things. The voice answered me, saying that my health would improve and that I would get a better understanding of life in the near future.

A few minutes later, the music stopped. I thought that the ceremony had just ended, so I stood up to go to my hut. I walked in front of Tao, an excellent singer, musician, and probably a shaman too. He was one of the few people to take part in the songs at the end of each ceremony and to take care of the fire for the entire night. He and Mariana are a couple that I would describe as extraordinary, as they exude perfect harmony.

Tao had just grabbed his guitar and began to strum the strings to let out a few melodic notes. He was sitting next to the shamans. There was an empty chair behind him, a few meters away. I sat on it. The voice inside me told me to stay there for a moment because I still needed to experience something. I had the curious impression that I had moved from one workshop to another to be taught different lessons. The voice told me that this lesson was about beauty and humility. It was, indeed, a magical moment. Each music note was a part of a whole which has no beginning or end. Even during its brief existence, it had its place in the universe. Without it, the notes before or after would not have existed. The melody and beauty that came from it would not have existed either. I drew the parallels with my life, that of my loved ones, then that of all human beings, of all other past, present and future creatures, and with all seemingly inanimate objects on Earth and elsewhere. Everything seemed to make sense. Everything was perfect. "What a wonderful feeling to be alive, here and now," I thought.

When the last song ended, Tao put his guitar down on the sand, against the trunk of a palm tree nearby. I went back to my hut. I walked in light steps, under the impression that I was floating on the ground. I felt that, my life, even though tiny in this infinite universe, has its importance. I felt loved and loving. I felt like I was part of something vast and extremely beautiful, probably for the first time in my life.

❋ ❋ ❋

When I woke up the next morning, I felt light in my head and in my body. I had a sensation of an ineffable peace. My thoughts were surprisingly clear. They didn't wander in every direction like they normally do upon waking up. I could give in to the moment with ease. The noises coming from the outside seemed almost harmonious. I jumped out of my hammock, quickly opened the mosquito net, and exited the hut. Outside, the light was gracious. Surprisingly, it was not hot and humid, it was just perfect.

I saw my friends at breakfast. They asked me if the ceremony went well. I answered affirmatively without expanding on it because I did not want to tell those who had visibly had a difficult evening that my night had ended so harmoniously.

When I went back to my hut, I thought about the events of the night before. A thought slowly began to torment me. "What do I need to do now? Have I reached the final destination? If I have, why am I so clearly the person that I was yesterday?" I did not feel that I had achieved omnipresence, omniscience, wisdom or purity. Animals did not stop in my path, they did not run from the four corners of the forest to salute me. I was just myself, perhaps a little more at peace, but fundamentally, I was the same person as I was the day before. "What do I have to do now? Do I still have to take part in the coming ceremonies? If I do, what for, with what attitude? To experience the same thing?" It didn't make a lot of sense.

In the afternoon, we participated in a ceremony that involved getting injected in the eye with an extract of a very spicy plant. Hunters mainly engage in this ancestral practice, named 'Sananga,' in order to increase their sight for the purpose of locating and following their animal prey more easily. Even though the dose injected into our eyes was significantly lower than that taken by hunters, the burning sensation was very intense.

During this ceremony, I met Marco, one of the members of the Russian camera crew. Of Italian descent, Marco is a reporter for a famous international newspaper. At the time we met, he had been living in Russia for many years. We shared a few words about the ceremony from the night before. I broadly shared my experience of death and rebirth. He was very excited. I also related my concerns regarding how to approach the next ceremonies.

"How to behave during the next ceremony is what worries me a little now, Marco."

"Adriano, if you want, you can ask our Portuguese translator to translate your questions to Ninawa. You take him to one side and ask him your questions. What do you think?"

Even though the thought of meeting face to face with the imposing chief shaman did not make me feel particularly at ease, I thought that my friend's proposition was opportune. I thanked him for his suggestion and gave him my approval. He promptly went to look for Sarah, the translator. When he came back, I shared my questions with Sarah, who assured me she was happy to help, and went to look for Ninawa. A few minutes later, she came back and told us that the chief shaman was waiting for us near the sacred tree, a few meters away from the hut in which the sananga ceremony had taken place.

Ninawa was leaning on the sacred tree, his hands in the pockets of his Bermuda shorts. He watched us walking towards him, then welcomed us with a broad smile. His forehead, cheeks, and forearms were covered in shamanic patterns. His calm force was reassuring. Sarah translated my questions and concerns about last night's ceremony to the chief shaman. Ninawa stared at me for a few moments. He did not seem to be surprised. Still with a smile on his face, he turned to Sarah and told her that some of us had a similar experience. He added that I now had to use the knowledge that I acquired during the ceremony to tackle the upcoming ones. Strangely, even though a part of me had wanted the chief shaman to tell me that I did not need to take part in the ceremonies anymore, that everything was as it ought to be, and that my life was now in the hands of angels that had organized everything, I was neither surprised nor disappointed. Maybe the explorer in me was not yet satisfied, or perhaps I needed to explore further and deeper inner realms with the help of ayahuasca.

However, a question had constantly haunted me since the morning. It became more and more pressing now that I was face to face with Ninawa: given that I listened to music through my headphones the night before to mask the horrible shamanic incantations, was my experience of death and rebirth last night caused or, even worse, completely fabricated by my desperate action? This possibility terrified me because if it turned out to be the case, I would have to face again the terrible visions and hypnotic sensations that haunted me. In other words, I would have to gather my courage and finally face my fears. Nevertheless, I decided not share my torments with the imposing chief shaman. I intuitively knew that he would have strongly advised against listening to music during ceremonies, and perhaps even reprimanded me for having had the audacity to dare it. He would have been right, and I knew it, for I myself was ashamed of my own behavior.

Nevertheless, just before thanking the chief shaman for his advice, and with a little hesitation and discomfort in my voice, I asked Sarah if I could ask Ninawa one last question. My request translated, Ninawa gave me a sign of approval with his head.

"Ninawa, why do you smile at me every time you hold the ayahuasca to me even though you don't smile at anyone else?"

Bursting out laughing and tipping his head slightly backwards, Ninawa answered without pausing:

"Oh, that's very simple! You smile at me, so I smile back at you!"

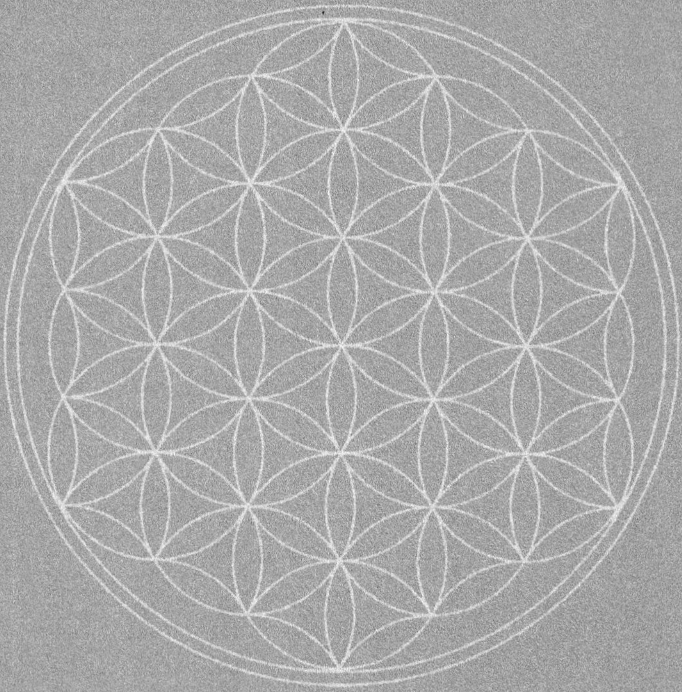

Observations and Reflections on Ayahuasca

Man is his own demon.
— Indian proverb

November 18, 2016

Three brief flute sounds signaled ten o'clock in the evening. Most of the participants were sitting around the sacred fire and had gathered their shamanic instruments and ornaments in front of them. Cathie, the British woman sitting to my left in the lotus position, had placed to her right a small wooden chair, which she had borrowed from inside the maloca. I thought it was an excellent idea to keep one's back straight under the influence of ayahuasca. I stood up and made my way to the ceremonial hut to take one for myself.

At the entrance, I realized that it was the first time that I entered the maloca since the ceremony during which the giant labyrinth had appeared. A few steps further in the maloca, I stopped for a moment, looked around and uttered a long and regretful sigh of nostalgia while remembering the events of those two nights when the flamboyant geometrical shapes had invaded my sky, when there had been no dark visions or hypnotic sensations yet. "Why isn't it the same anymore?" I questioned, mentally, "It is surely because of the new ayahuasca brew, I know that. So, why not serve the drink that tastes like orange and sweet alcohol again?" There certainly was a reason for that, but I was simply unable to grasp it.

There was no empty chair in the maloca. The only two were occupied by an old villager smoking tobacco and a mother with her child asleep on her lap. I returned to my mat. I asked Cathie if I could borrow her chair while she was not using it. She approved by smiling and nodding.

After drinking the contents of the glass that Ninawa held out to me, I sat on my chair with my back straight like an iron rod, hoping to remain on it all night, no matter what happened. After about twenty minutes, I started to feel the effects of the concoction. I experienced the usual sensations such as heavy head, confused thoughts and intense fatigue. The visions also followed in a succession of geometrical shapes and vivid colors that constantly metamorphosed. It was dark, barely lit by the glow of a quarter of the waning moon. The sight of the hoard of shamans pressed against each other, uttering incantations at the top of their lungs in perfect synchronization, sent shivers down my spine.

It was the first time, however, that I was able to contemplate their performance in detail. At the same time during the previous ceremonies, I had already either collapsed on my mat or run away. I observed the scene that had been unknown until that point: the tireless flames of the sacred fire in the center of the shamanic circle desperately trying to warm and protect the participants already slumped on the ground; the villagers adorned with unusual ornaments staring at the shamans with stoic faces; the women of the village wearing long and dark dresses, arms crossed, resembling ancient statues; the children covered in strange paintings lurking silently just outside the circle; the annoying howls of the village's dogs further darkening the scene, which had become unbearable.

After about an hour concentrating on my breathing and looking for stars in a sky that had become dark and gloomy, I was exhausted. "What should I see now? What should I feel? How should I act? Will there be a peaceful end? Will there be an end at all? When? And why?" Looking at the white sand below my feet, it was nearly impossible not to collapse to the ground. The feeling was only too familiar. "Should I now lie on the sand and let the visions carry me away? Will there be a divine scheme beyond them? Is this the path that I must follow? My friends lying on the ground do not seem to have the same dilemma————But wait—No. Why must I go through hell? None of this makes any sense at all." At that moment, however, despite the terrifying visions that started haunting me, I realized that it wasn't really them that overwhelmed me the most, but rather, it was the suffocating feeling of losing control of my thoughts, of my mental abilities, of my mind; *that* was the thing I was not able to surrender to. As soon as I closed my eyes, I had the horrible sensation that I was sucked into a never-ending long and narrow tunnel. I was under the impression that, at any moment, I was going to enter an infernal whirlwind from which I could never escape and where I would lose myself, never to return. I wondered how my friends were able to deal with that suffocating and hypnotic sensation, or if they had to, but for myself, I simply could not do it. I was terrified.

With Herculean effort, I stood up and walked to my hut. Three villagers with large headdresses were sitting on the wooden steps in front of the door. I ignored them. It did not matter to me anymore. I easily found my phone, put my headphones on my ears, played the music, and lay down in the tent. I was in complete control of the process. I just needed to repeat again each step in a precise sequence. However, once the music started playing, not only was I increasingly nervous, but my heartbeat accelerated dramatically. In addition, the hypnosis created by the shamanic incantations drained all my energy away. My mind begged me to collapse to the ground and surrender with all my soul. However, I could not do it.

In the hours that followed, I tried everything I could to stay awake: focusing on my breathing, sitting down with my back straight, uttering positive thoughts, praying to the gods, forcing myself to vomit, lying down, walking, begging the sky, praying again, begging for forgiveness, walking again, and praying once more. All these helped, but none was effective enough. At some point, amongst the tireless nightmarish visions and still with my eyes closed, I saw a dark red light emanating from the center of my heart, which was racing and aching terribly to such an extent that I was convinced I was going to have a heart attack.

I must have lost consciousness shortly after because when I reopened my eyes, I was lying down on the doorstep of the hut. Veronica was leaning forward and staring into my eyes. She looked concerned. The movement of her lips indicated that she was repeating the same sounds, but I could not hear them. "She is surely worried and asking if I am okay," I thought. After a few unsuccessful attempts to utter a sound, I eventually succeeded in telling her that I was exhausted, but everything was fine. With a big smile that deeply warmed my heart, she answered: "Oh, that's great! Adriano, when you're feeling better, come and join us, okay?" I answered with a smile. Before I passed out again, I saw Veronica make a few steps towards the shamanic circle.

When I regained consciousness, I was feeling better. The effects of ayahuasca had faded. I straightened up and sat on the door-step. Harmonious music had replaced the incantations. I decided to join my friends. I needed to exert a lot of effort to stand up and join the circle. When I finally reached it, I noticed that most of the participants were still lying on the ground. The evening had clearly been difficult for them too. A handful of villagers were dancing chaotically in the center of the circle around the glowing embers. I clumsily crossed the circle and took part in the snake dance. While trying to move my body to the rhythm of the music, I remembered the words that the soft and deep voice had told me the night before: "You can recreate what you are feeling now at any moment if you wish to." However, despite all my efforts, I was not able to relive the wonderful emotions that I had felt barely twenty-four hours prior.

As Bernard stated in a humorous way just before my first cer-emony, ayahuasca is well-known for its 'maceration' process. Once consumed, it macerates inside the stomach and in most cases causes vomiting one or two hours later, which is considered to be positive in the shamanic experience. Stories relating visions of snakes or other reptilian creatures coming out of the mouth when vomit-ing are common. While awkwardly treading the sand around the fire, I had a disturbing feeling that the villagers were watching me. "They surely know that the maceration is still happening inside me, that the 'ayahuasca snake' has not yet emerged from my entrails,"

I thought in discomfort.

When the Sun appeared in the sky, I returned to my hut to find sleep.

❄ ❄ ❄

The next morning, I woke up with a lot of questions on my mind. I wondered why the ceremony the night before was so negative. "Why did I not experience something similar or better than the ceremony before? What is the absurd logic that orchestrates ayahuasca ceremonies?" While remembering certain Buddhist murals that represent life according to lower and higher realms and the passage through death, I could not help but draw the parallel between these scenes—which are sordid to say the least—and my experiences with ayahuasca. "Should the path of spirituality, which operates through a change of consciousness, necessarily go through darkness or hell? Do we have to go through the agonizing experience of death to elevate ourselves spiritually? Can we elevate ourselves *only* if we have gone through the Inferno? If so, what have we possibly done as a human race to deserve such a sordid fate?" None of that were making sense.

Tired of all of these questions without answers, absorbed in my memories of the night before, and still feeling intoxicated, I left my hut. The left side of my chest was still hurting. I was under the impression that I was in a dream. The images that I was seeing were wobbly, as if I was looking at the world on the screen of a television that was on its last legs.

On the way to the canteen, I met Asil. Asil is from Austria and nearly forty years old. After having been an international businessman for many years in the computer industry, he amassed a small fortune by selling the shares of his company to his associates. Since then, he has traveled the world to lead shamanic ceremonies amongst other things. I do not know the details of his shamanic studies, but he is clearly talented and knowledgeable in the field. He and Rory have been friends for a long time. Also, besides having an infinite patience and a great ability to stay calm in the most difficult situations, Asil has a great sense of humor.

After painstakingly gathering my thoughts, I shared my difficulties regarding the previous night's ceremony with my friend. Strangely, while relating the events, I realized that I was no longer ashamed to share my inner battles. They started to sound somehow natural. My friend told me that most of us had experienced a difficult night. I asked him if he thought that ayahuasca was demonic. With a compassionate smile, he stated that it was indeed possible for dark entities to appear before certain participants, especially during particularly intense and difficult ceremonies. I did not dig deeper into the question because I intuitively knew that it was pointless. I knew that my issue, my battles, had nothing to do with dark spirits. However, sharing my worries and questions with Asil and freeing myself from certain emotions made me feel surprisingly better.

Somehow, I did not feel the need to ask most of the questions I had prepared in my mind. They were not *that* important anymore. I only had one remaining question: why do we actually take part in ayahuasca ceremonies? In other words, what is their aim in the progression of the human soul? Based on my experiences and thoughts on the effects of the fearsome brew, the most plausible explanation that I could think of was that it introduced a sort of 'evil entity' to those who consume it to force them to look in the depths of their soul for the strength that was needed to expel the entity. In other words, it would be a sort of training that aimed to develop willpower for the purpose of manifesting the divine light in us. In some ways, this theory reminded me of vaccination. Known empirically since ancient times, vaccination consists of putting the organism in contact with very small doses of viruses or bacteria in order to force the body to create the defenses needed against all future attacks by pathogens. With that thought, my ambition was to get any advice that could prove to be effective in order to never succumb to ayahuasca's 'demonic attacks' again.

I asked Asil how I should behave during ayahuasca ceremonies and carefully noted his advice. This is a summary: do not lie down, keep your eyes open, keep your back straight, focus on your breathing, stare at the stars in the sky while breathing in deeply and slowly through your nose and breathing out of your mouth, stare at the fire in the middle of the shamanic circle, pray, recite a mantra, sing quietly, and, this is very important: *stay inside the shamanic circle!* Also, the one thing that one should never do is be overcome by fear, panic, or anxiety. Ironically, the last two pieces of advice given by Asil were precisely what I did not follow during the previous ceremonies, which made me smile sadly while remembering my past actions. Asil added that as a beginner, and until one gain a certain ability to navigate the meanders of the complex world of ayahuasca, one had to avoid staying still for too long. He recommended moving the spine gently and slowly if the urge to sleep became unbearable.

Even though I was very happy to obtain help when I needed the most, I did not expect to receive such seemingly simple advice. I initially believed that Asil would talk about techniques to protect oneself from evil visions, mention the aspect of monstrous entities, and perhaps go into sacred and hitherto secret spiritual rituals. Instead, he kept his feet firmly on the ground and gave me simple, practical, and yet useful pieces of advice which do seem essential to anyone who seriously wants to work with ayahuasca.

I then realized that my theory about the demonic aspect of the sacred plant was foolish, to say the least. "What is this 'demon' that I accuse of being the cause of my troubles during ceremonies?" I asked myself, "What is this unknown force? Does it come from within me? Why was it completely unknown to me until very recently? Why do I know so little about myself? Who am I really?" I came to the conclusion that if there was such a demon or dark and negative force in the shamanic experience with ayahuasca, it could only be inside me, which made me wonder for a few moments. At that point, and just before my mind wandered in the why, how, and where this evil would come from, I stopped. That quest was not important, at least not immediately. How I was going to behave during the next ceremony was the issue at hand, and I had to focus my energy on that.

After a few more moments lost in my thoughts, I wondered if the dark visions that tormented me were not created by my subconscious. "Could they be the result of fears deeply rooted in me, perhaps from a distant past?" No matter the answer to that question, it became clear that I had to face my inner demons soon or later. More specifically, I had to face the nightmarish visions during the next ceremony to understand what they were trying to tell me.

I tapped Asil's shoulder while smiling at him. He smiled back and asked if I had any more questions.

"Thank you so much, brother. I think that if I manage to follow all of your advice, I should have a chance of doing better this time," I answered.

Most of the people I had met who claim to be spiritual have a common behavior pattern: they tend not to have a good grasp on reality, which I find disturbing. Asil, however, though clearly at ease and very experienced with the world of spirituality, is down to earth, which I admired a lot. He is the kind of person who does not hesitate to get to the bottom of things in order to understand the mechanisms of human behavior and the world surrounding him. During many discussions we had with Scott, Rory, and other participants, Asil always encouraged us to give our opinions and share our respective experiences in order to improve our understanding of the spiritual worlds.

❄ ❄ ❄

The same day, at the beginning of the afternoon, the organizers had planned healing sessions. They were to be given individually by the shamans from the neighboring villages that had joined Ninawa for the festival. I asked the organizers if it would be possible for me to have Ninawa as my healer, but no one knew when he was going to arrive. As I still had sharp pains in my chest, I decided to take part in the healing sessions without waiting for Ninawa's arrival.

I entered the maloca, took a few steps and sat down on one of the round straw mats on the floor. The hut was empty, I was apparently the first person to attend the healing sessions. On my right, on another straw mat just a few steps away was placed the small wooden statue that stood next to the jar of ayahuasca in each ceremony. The thought of grimacing at it crossed my mind, but a feeling of reverence—and surely, fear of the consequences of doing so—overtook it.

A few minutes later, a shaman dressed in a long, white and bright tunic and wearing a high and multicolored headdress entered the maloca. He sat opposite me, on the other side of the small wooden table that separated us. He was probably in his late thirties. His peaceful smile and special aura soothed me immediately. The geometrical paintings that covered his forehead, prominent and high cheekbones and forearms up to the middle of his biceps emphasized his majestic appearance.

As it is the custom during such shamanic practices, he introduced himself by telling me his name, the tribe that he belonged to, and how long he had been a shaman for. Once the shaman's words translated by one of the organizers who had just joined him, I also briefly introduced myself and explained why I came to see him. After thoroughly examining me with his piercing gaze, he stood up, walked behind me, then sucked air through his tobacco pipe that he had just lit, and breathed out the smoke with great force all around me while muttering incantations. He then put a small handful of tobacco-based powder inside a long tube that looked like a bird's bone and which was adorned with small ornaments, then put one of the mouthpieces to the entrance of one of my nostrils. After remembering that I could only breathe through my mouth from this moment until the process was complete, I signaled to him that I was ready to receive the preparation. He blew air through the other end of the tube, then did the same for my other nostril.

Blowing this powder, called 'rapé', into the nostrils is a common practice in shamanic practices. Rapé is a mixture of roasted Peruvian tobacco powder, sacred ceremonial ash, and medicinal plants, prepared by a shaman under the protection of healing prayers. The blow of rapé has to be done in each nostril, alternately, with a relatively strong and dry blow to—as I was told—penetrate the subtle channels.

A 'lucky' coincidence had made me take part in a rapé session the day before with Ninawa. The chief shaman had earned the fierce reputation of not being very subtle with his rapé blow. As I was sitting in front of him, with a half-smile, I had mentally prepared myself to receive the mixture. When he sent the powder through one of my nostrils with a dry and strong blow, I had to use control that I did not know I possessed to remain seated and present the austere-looking shaman my other nostril. Having received the same amount of powder in my nostril with the same strength, I stood up with a lot of effort while holding onto one of the maloca's beams. After respectfully showing a sign of gratitude to the chief shaman, I turned around, then staggered through the hut from beam to beam until I reached a small wooden trunk placed by a charitable soul who clearly knew very well the aftereffects of 'Ninawa's blow'. Besides the intense burning sensation in my nostrils and up to the back of my throat and the sudden and strong nausea, I was under the impression that the ground was shaking dangerously beneath my feet, so much so that it was impossible for me to keep my balance even though I was sitting. A few minutes later, I had to empty my stomach at the foot of one of the palm trees behind the maloca.

By now, the shaman, who saw that I was physically weak, took care of me by sending the rapé into my nostrils with a soft blow. I continued to breathe through my mouth for a few more moments for the desired effects of this age-old practice to be felt, then blew my nose a few times before starting breathing normally. The shaman subsequently confirmed that my heart and throat were tired, but that I would soon feel better. He added that I could take part in the upcoming ceremony and that I should notice a significant difference in the coming hours. I respectfully thanked him and left the maloca.

On the way back to my hut, I noticed that I was already feeling better. Curiously, I felt less intoxicated and my thoughts were clearer.

In the evening to come, though still exhausted, I was to take part in the ceremony.

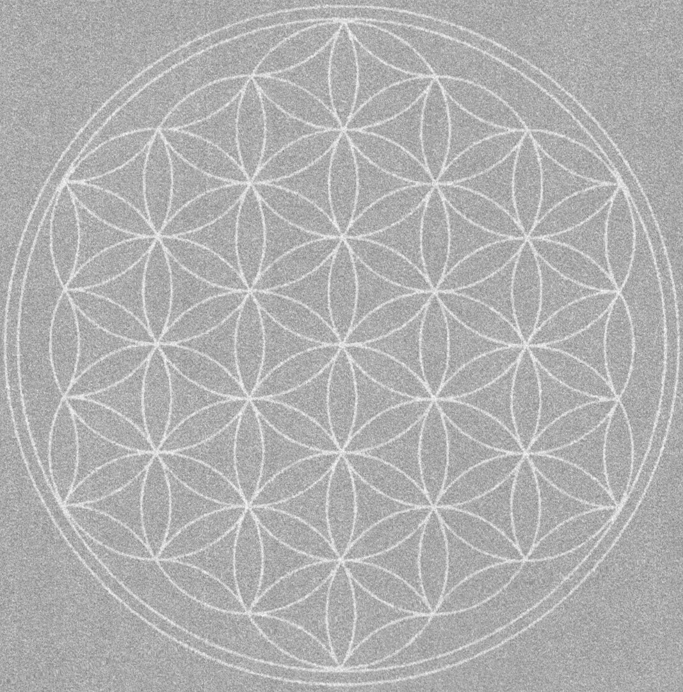

A Ceremony Without Ayahuasca

God does not belong to the scientist, nor to the logician;
He belongs to the poets, to the realm of dreams;
He is the symbol of Beauty, Beauty itself.
—Paul Gauguin

November 19, 2016

In the evening, Yogesh asked me if I was planning on participating in the ceremony. I was lying in my hammock, still exhausted. My head was heavy and a feeling of intoxication prevented me from making a quick decision. Furthermore, the pain on the left side of my chest was still present. After a few moments lost in my thoughts, I told Yogesh that I was not sure yet and I would consider it.

After leaving the hut, I exchanged a few words with my friends who were nearby. During the discussion, I realized that I was not the only one in this state. The long nocturnal ceremonies interrupted by torrid and humid days during which most of us only slept very little deprived us of a large part of our energy. Yet, the thought of missing a ceremony was in no way tempting. My time in this jungle with the shamans was limited. I needed to benefit as much as I could from it. Therefore, I decided to take part in the ceremony, but without drinking ayahuasca. I knew that this practice was generally not allowed by the organizers. However, my intention was noble. It was not to observe and judge my friends when they would be under the influence of ayahuasca while I would be sober, but to try and understand the shamanic practices that caused me so much woe. "At the end of tonight," I thought, "I will know if I should continue taking part in the upcoming ceremonies or if I should pack my bags and escape as soon as possible." The Russian camera crew was to leave the village one or two days later. I knew that from a logistic and legal standpoint it would have been very difficult, perhaps impossible, to take off with them on the helicopter, but I found myself several times imagining being lifted up into the air from the vast terrain behind the maloca.

As evening arrived, I sat on one of the tree trunks that had been placed along the circle by the villagers to be used as low stools. Dusk had just fallen. The shamans had not arrived yet. Half an hour later, the rest of the participants, the villagers, and the shamans took their seat. The ayahuasca was served. No one asked me why I did not join the line as I usually did. Perhaps, and as it is normally the case for me as well, everyone was absorbed by their own concerns or wanted to focus on themselves in order to fully benefit from the upcoming experience just before taking ayahuasca.

After about twenty minutes in total silence, the shamans began their chants. It was the first time that I could watch them straighten up on their chair, readjust their tunic, headdress and shamanic ornaments. Some of them looked at each other, but almost all of them knew the movements that had been repeated thousands of times. After gently clearing their throats a few times, they started uttering their incantations. Their majestic beauty and perfect synchronization sent shivers up and down my spine. Together, they transmitted an almost superhuman power. It was almost as if their ancestors were in front of the shamans to orchestrate the performance. "Why did these beings chose to embody shamans here, in the deep jungle?" I thought, "Did they consciously and voluntarily decide to come to our aid?" Through these age-old practices, which they visibly had acquired complete control of, they showed infinite compassion and unconditional love towards us, towards total strangers. While lowering my head, staring at the sand, I was somehow sad about my own state, that of my friends, and that of humanity. "What have we possibly done to end up the way we are now? How did we get so lost as the human race, as a society, as individuals, and as souls?"

Still seated in the same position, spine straight on the sky-Earth axis, I listened to the chants for a long time. Out of respect for my friends, I did not stare at them or made mental comments. After about two hours, they were almost all lying on the ground. I felt sympathy for what must have been happening in their heads, for the journey that they were going on. I greatly admired their control, strength, perseverance and fearlessness.

As time went on, I felt more and more that everything was perfect, in harmony, as it should be. Although the incantations were powerful and impressive, they were far from the satanic chants that I had accused them during the previous ceremonies, when I was under the influence of ayahuasca and unreasonably panicked.

The more time went on, the more I found beauty and wisdom in these ancestral practices. I did not understand the meaning of the incantations or their mysterious effects on the human psyche, but they seemed right to me. "What is the relation between sound and the human soul?" I thought. "Why is ayahuasca clearly so important in this process? Am I witnessing a restructuring or a reprogramming of the mind? If so, is that essential for our species' survival? Why do I find it so difficult to face these incantations, whereas my friends seem to be able to do so without apparent struggle? Is it because I have been so damaged by the teachings of our modern societies which are solely based on intellectual education?" My questions regarding human nature, its future, and its place in the universe went on for a long time.

The physical pain in my heart faded progressively as I watched the scene around me. I was in peace. I gave in to the moment. I was happy.

Tao and Mariana, the young couple, whom I found very united and harmonious, stayed awake for the whole night. Tao attended the sacred fire. Near the end of the ceremony, with a long wooden stick, he pushed a pile of embers away from the fire to gather them and make a big heart in the sand, which made the few participants who were still awake smile. Some of them stood up, took a few steps towards the fire, and stayed there for a long time contemplating the glows of the incandescent shape in the sand. Mariana took care of some struggling participants almost all night. I was extremely surprised by this harmonious couple's behavior under the influence of ayahuasca. They had clearly achieved full control of their emotions and thoughts. They had surely acquired a very good understanding of the work of the mind and soul during ayahuasca ceremonies. I never really conversed with them during my stay in the Amazon, but only very briefly. Maybe I was too preoccupied with my own issues, or perhaps they were too busy taking care of other participants. I do not know the reason, but I regret it today.

Once the last chant ended, the shamans remained still on their chair. The silence became strangely heavy. The participants also became still. Some shamans stood up to grab their musical instrument. Others took a few steps to stretch their legs, while some others took a sip of water from the bottle next to the ayahuasca jar. I smiled. Once they returned to their seat, they began to play their favorite song, accompanied by their guitars, flutes and drums. What a display, what a performance, what a heavenly harmony. I felt tears rolling down my cheeks.

Some of the women of the village took a small leap and crossed the circle to embody the ayahuasca snake in its sacred and graceful dance. Everything had a rare finesse and lightness. Some of the participants came back to life with a certain ease, as if they had repeated the same sequence a thousand times. Others sat up with difficulty, like they had woken up from a long dream. The majority of them stayed on the ground, surely to complete their journey. A few minutes later, a small number of participants joined the dancers. I did the same. I loved this dance. In shamanic circles, it is said that the ayahuasca spirit rejoices in the performance of the snake moving gracefully and tirelessly around the sacred fire.

After a few more songs, I returned to my hut. I was bathing in delight and in great peace. I then knew without doubt that I was the sole author of my fears.

With a new perspective, I was already looking forward to taking part in the next ayahuasca ceremony.

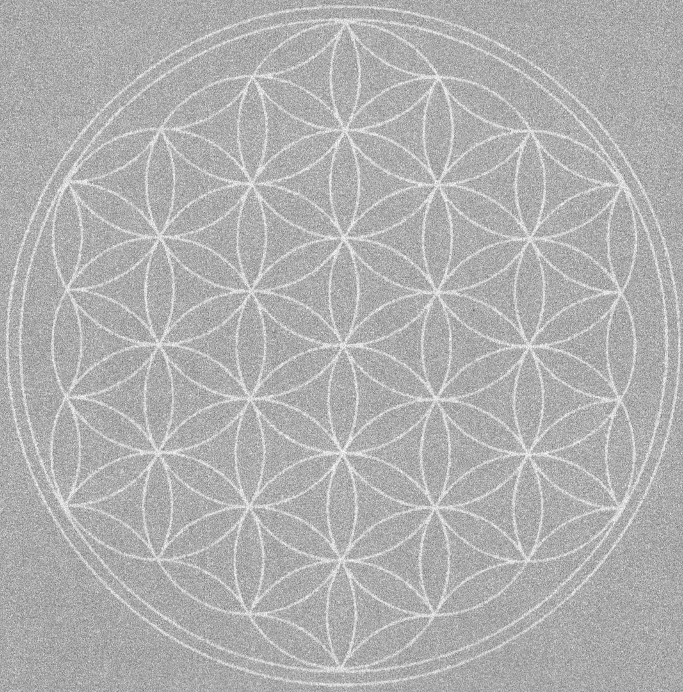

The Control of Emotions

If you want to be free from your emotions, you need to have true and immediate knowledge of your emotions.
—Arnaud Desjardins

Legend has it the inhabitants of a village were very ill, and a shaman named Kambó had done everything in his power to cure them. All the known medicinal herbs had been used, but none of them had been effective enough. On a certain day and under the effect of ayahuasca, Kambó entered the forest and was visited by a great spirit carrying a frog in his hands. He extracted a white secretion from the frog, then taught the shaman how to use it to cure his people. When he returned to the village, Kambó was able to cure the inhabitants by following the instructions he had received. As a result, the indigenous Amazon people began to use the frog's secretion to stay in good health.

❄ ❄ ❄

November 21, 2016

It must have been nine o'clock in the morning. Stomachs still empty, we were all gathered in front of the maloca. The organizers and shamans had planned for us to participate in a kambó ceremony.

Kambó is a poison that is secreted by the giant Phyllomedusa bicolor frog. Shamans have used it in purification and healing rituals for a very long time. By following a particular technique, the poison triggers a detoxification process once it is applied on the skin of a patient or of those who participate in a kambó ceremony. Kambó also contains substances that have antibacterial and antiviral functions, stimulate the immune system, reduce inflammations, and improve blood flow.

I did not know what kambó was, but my friends, who took part in such ceremonies during the previous festivals, burst out laughing while recounting tales of past sessions that they found amusing and which started to worry me, to say the least. I grimaced when I learned that the effects mentioned included nausea and uncontrollable vomiting. "Until you vomit, the shamans will keep on giving you more kambó!" Bernard told me while laughing heartily.

A high increase of blood pressure, swelling of the head, notably the lips, eyes, and sometimes forehead, and, in a lot of cases, uncontrollable diarrhea are amongst the other notorious effects that are generally reported. It became obvious to me that, just like the yogis in India, the shamans greatly value the role of body detoxification in their practices.

One of the organizers told us that Ninawa had just received a 'kambó frog' from a neighboring village. Driven by curiosity, some of us quickly crossed the path to the chief shaman's hut. Ninawa was seated in front of the doorstep. A metal bucket was placed on the ground a meter to his right. Banana leaves were used as the lid. After the respectful customary greetings, one of the organizers walked towards the bucket, leaned over and meant to lift one of the banana leaves. Very excited and without thinking, we all took a step in his direction, looking at the mysterious container. It did not take long for Ninawa to realize why we were suddenly so enthusiastic, or rather, why we were all gathered in front of his doorstep.

With a smile on his face, the chief shaman stood up, grabbed the bucket with one hand, lifted it up to his hips, then let one of the banana leaves fall on the ground. When I leaned over the container after carving a path for myself between my friends, I was greatly surprised by the size of the frog. Crouching, the amphibian must have been ten to twelve centimeters long. It had impressively wide adhesive discs on the end of its fingers and toes. And, with its bright green color, still and wide eyes, and absolute stillness, it looked like a big toy made from shiny plastic. With a confident movement, Ninawa put his hand in the bucket, slid it underneath the frog, then lifted it to shoulder height while putting the bucket back on the ground. The frog had not moved an inch. The vividly green color that covered its entire upper body ended just below its head. Its stomach and the entire underside of its body were a yellowish color, or maybe cream.

I learned that for the frog to secrete the poison, you first need to attach a piece of string around each limb, then gently pull on each of them so its entire body is flat on the ground. This is normally done by two or three people. Then, all you have to do is gently rub its back with a small branch to generate enough stress for the frog to feel that it is in danger and release the poison, the kambó. Once the necessary amount has been obtained, the frightened frog is released into the forest safe and sound.

Ninawa delicately placed the frog at the bottom of the bucket. It still had not moved one iota.

When we reached the sacred tree, ten large buckets filled with water mixed with sweet corn juice had been placed at the foot of the tree. Each of us had to drink two liters of it before beginning the ceremony. As we were all going to vomit soon after the poison was placed on our bodies, drinking a large amount of this liquid beforehand would make the task considerably easier and lower the stress on the stomach and esophagus.

Ninawa was surrounded by his fellow shamans. After a few welcoming words, they opened the ceremony with beautiful and traditional songs accompanied by guitars and drums. The chief shaman then gave us the instructions to see the kambó ceremony through. Finally, with a broad smile, he invited us to place ourselves in front of the buckets to drink the sweet corn juice preparation.

I did not hesitate before joining the line. As I had quite significant experience with certain yoga techniques to detoxify my body, I was very curious. Hernan was standing in front of me, Yogesh and Aesha were just behind. Plastic cups had been placed near the buckets. Our first task was to drink six or seven cups of sweet corn juice each, without pausing, which I did without too much difficulty. Then, we had to quickly present ourselves one by one to one of the shamans who, with the help of the incandescent end of an incense stick, would burn the upper layer of the epidermis in the spot chosen by each of us with the aim of applying the poison secreted by the frog, the kambó. The secretion directly applied to the burn would be directly absorbed by the blood flow.

The art of this ancestral technique is to correctly gage the number of burns needed for the poison to have the desired effect. If the number of burns is not enough, one would need to quickly be burned more times and increase the amount of kambó to trigger the vomiting effect. If the number of burns is too high, the blood pressure and the vomiting could make the experience painful, or even dangerous[1].

When my turn came, the shaman asked me where I wanted to be burned. I told him the outside of my left shoulder. Some people chose inside the forearm, an ankle, or a part of the back. He also asked me if this was my first time. I acquiesced, slightly nervous. Normally, the shaman should burn a novice two or three times. However, after examining me with his gaze, he burned me five times with the end of his incense stick. Unexpectedly, the pain was quite mild. Then, with a small branch, he applied a whitish paste to each of the burns with a quick movement.

By the time the third wound was covered, my heartbeat had increased sharply. Once all wounds covered, I took a few steps towards the dense forest, then felt the blood pressure in my head increase to a point that I was under the impression that it had grown tenfold. I had the horrible feeling that I was going to faint. I bent forward while pressing with one hand against an enormous tree trunk on the ground and quickly placed the other hand on my knee not to

---

1. It goes without saying that, like with ayahuasca, sanaga, rapé, and all other shamanic techniques, it is essential that each participant inform the shamans and organizers of their physical and mental health *before* going on these adventures.

lose balance. I felt horribly nauseous, but even though my stomach was contracting, I was unable to vomit. A villager who had followed me was watching me closely. Out of fear that he would order for more burns and because I was convinced that I could not take another ounce of kambó in my system, I quickly pushed two fingers into my throat to make myself vomit[1]. Without going into details, I can attest to the results of this ancestral technique. Once I had completely emptied my stomach, the villager gently tapped my shoulder. Smiling and visibly satisfied, he rejoined the shamans. My heartbeat returned to a normal rate after a few minutes. I had to rest for a while on the tree trunk behind me to catch my breath and regain all my senses.

The waiting line in front of the shamans was still long. After about half an hour and just before taking the path to my hut, I looked around me to see where my friends were. I was surprised when I saw the face of one of my fellow participants. It was so deformed that it took me a while to recognize who she was. Her lips, eyelids, and forehead had swollen to worrying proportions. While trying to comfort her, the people around were clearly struggling to contain their laughter. I am slightly ashamed to admit that I had to look away a few times to contain my chucking. Her face looked like a caricature from a funny cartoon. As this young woman had a genuinely good heart, she often laughed about her temporary misfortune during the days that followed. The swelling disappeared totally after three days.

The same ceremony took place again a few days later. However,

---

1. It is to be noted, however that forcing oneself to vomit when doing kambó is not recommended.

considering the fatigue caused by the ayahuasca ceremonies, the other activities planned by the organizers, and the torrid heat of the jungle—and the mosquitoes, I did not take part.

❄ ❄ ❄

In the evening, while walking towards the shamanic circle and reflecting on my thoughts from the night before during the ceremony without ayahuasca, a thought began to torment me. All my analyses and theories about shamanism, ayahuasca, spirituality, and human nature were intellectually entertaining, but I knew that only experience could bring me concrete results and knowledge. I would need to go much deeper into the shamanic experience with ayahuasca, go through its meanders, and give in to its will. Regardless of the difficulties that would present themselves during the upcoming ceremony, I could *not* avoid it anymore. It was time to face my fears. That meant no more headphones in my ears, no more running away to my hut, no more excuses. I would have to be strong.

Ayahuasca was served as usual. I felt the first effects after about twenty minutes. The slightest whisper uttered by the participants, as soft as they may have been, invaded the space. An array of brightly colored and violent shapes put on a show in front of my impassive eyes. I kept my back straight, seated on a tree trunk deeply rooted in the sand, with my hands flat on my knees. The expected visions arrived, bringing along the sensations of hypnosis and mental imprisonment. Contrary to the previous ceremonies, however, I did not fight them. I watched them parade in front of me, one by one, without judging them, without getting involved. I was quite surprised to notice that the deeper I breathed, the more I was able to remain calm and relaxed, the weaker they became. I felt that I could have almost controlled them. Probably out of fear to start a process that I would have had no control over, I did not dare it.

Instead of beginning the chants like they normally do, the shamans asked us to stand up and form a large circle around the fire and to hold each other's hands. Once the circle formed, the incantations began. Although the power that came out of the shamans was as phenomenal and crushing as it was during the previous ceremonies, we all stayed on our feet, hand in hand. The shamans surely wanted to show us that it was possible to keep control of our mind under the effect of ayahuasca. I then realized that I was not the only one having difficulties, which somehow comforted me.

After a never-ending succession of chants, I was beginning to struggle to stay on my feet. I was almost constantly looking at the sky while breathing deeply. Just looking at the ground gave me vertigo and irresistible urge to lie in deep slumber on the smooth and comfortable sand. Every time the shamans finished a chant, I silently prayed for the next one not to start. However, although I was having a lot of trouble keeping my mind together, I was satisfied by the fact that I had not yet succumbed to the visions and feelings of hypnosis. I certainly had not gained total control of my thoughts and emotions, but the result seemed promising.

The chants did not last as long as during the previous ceremony. Soon after they ended, the music started. I joined the villagers who were already gathering around the fire. Dancing seemed to be an ideal way to stay awake the whole night without succumbing to the intoxication and fatigue caused by the ayahuasca. Every time a song ended, I silently summoned the next one by breathing deeply while staring at the stars which were slowly sneaking behind the clouds.

After about an hour mechanically following the steps of the villagers who were prancing in front of me to embody the ayahuasca snake, a thought suddenly crossed my mind: "Watch your heartbeat." Was it an internal protection mechanism that warned me that my heartbeat had accelerated to worrying speeds? Was it a fear that emerged from my unconscious? Was it an evil spirit that, knowing the effect that ayahuasca had on my mind, generated the fear inside of me in an insidious manner? I never found out. At that moment, I was feeling like a stranger in my body. I could not feel my heartbeat. To be honest, I could not feel anything in my body; I could not feel my feet, my legs, my heart, or even fatigue. I only took part in the dance not to collapse on the ground, not to give in to the visions and hypnotic effects of ayahuasca, and not to escape once again. It was a seemingly foolproof plan. By dancing non-stop around the sacred fire, I counted on the snake of the sacred plant to carry me through the night and take me to a safe land in the morning, illustrious vanquisher of my inner demons, conqueror of my fears.

I then placed my hand on my chest. My heart was beating regularly, perhaps a little quicker than normal, but considering the effort that the dance required under the effect of ayahuasca, I had nothing to worry about. However, from then on, I started to watch my heartbeat closely. At one point, after I closed my eyes, I saw a thread of red light forming and moving at great speed in my chest. The vision began to become obsessive. I was convinced that my heart was racing. I was terribly afraid. "Oh gosh… It's beating very quickly… Too quickly," I thought while nervously treading the sand beneath my feet. I exited the shamanic circle and tried to vomit, but to no avail. I then went back to my seat amongst the other participants. I was convinced that my heart was going to burst inside me.

During our group discussions between the two ceremonies, we were told time and again not to hesitate to call for help if the experience with ayahuasca became too intense or uncontrollable. I had never considered doing so up to that point, surely out of pride.

I noticed that Veronica, the young British woman, was standing close by. I told her that I needed help and asked her to quickly get a doctor, which she rushed to do. A few minutes later, she came back with a shaman. She was a rather short woman who looked to be in her late seventies. She was wearing a white tunic and headdress, as well as several ceremonial ornaments, as is customary for shamans. She seemed gentle and affectionate. Deep peace and calm strength emanated from her round and bright eyes. The contrast between her long white hair and her dark skin, which was deeply wrinkled by the Amazonian sun, made her look pure and noble. She spoke to me in Portuguese, but I could not understand. Through gestures, I tried to tell her what was wrong with me, but it was difficult to communicate. I asked Veronica to find a translator, which she did promptly.

Through the translator, I finally communicated my pain and concerns to the noble woman wearing the large headdress. She then stood in front of me, stared into my eyes for what seemed a long time, turned to the translator and said: "He is in this state because he is scared." Although what she had just said was all too familiar to me, this time, it was different. I felt that the message was directed at my soul. It was probably the first time that I found myself face to face with my ancestral fears. Realizing the great importance of this truth, I sighed deeply while looking in turn at Veronica, the translator, and the shaman, then replied: "Oh yes… I am scared… You are *so* right." Veronica put her hand on my shoulder and told me that I was now in good hands and that everything would be fine, then returned to the circle.

I was now alone with the shaman. While uttering harmonic incantations, with her right hand she outlined large circles around my head, shoulders, torso, in front of my chest, and a few centimeters from my heart. I closed my eyes to avoid being distracted by the movements. She then placed both hands on the top of my skull and blew air between them from her mouth with great vigor. I saw the inside of my body as if it was an immense cathedral. A bright white light infiltrated its roof, went through a large golden clock hanging in the middle of the cathedral, and lit up each of its corners. The brightness of the light was in perfect harmony with the blows of the mysterious woman with the angel feathers. The strongest blows lit up the entire space. Every time she caught her breath, the cathedral abruptly darkened. The only thought that I had on my mind was to let go and trust her. During this process, I was under the impression that my fears were swept away, that my heavy burdens were leaving me. I knew that everything was as it should be, I knew that everything was perfect. I felt light and soothed.

After bathing in euphoria for a long time, the shaman stopped, took two steps back, and asked me if I was feeling better. I put my hand on my heart. It was beating regularly. Unexpectedly, the pain had disappeared. I smiled at the shaman and thanked her very respectfully. She smiled at me and rejoined her fellow shamans on the other side of the circle.

I returned to my seat with a certain ease. Once sitting down, I watched the shamans, the villagers, the sky, and the landscape for about ten minutes, then I felt exhausted. The only thing that I wanted to do was lie on the ground. I fought the temptation for some time, but it proved to be stronger than my will. Much stronger. As my eyelids became too heavy, I looked around me one last time before lying down, thinking that I was going to find deep sleep. However, as soon as I shut my eyes, I felt tormented for no apparent reason. Random thoughts, seemingly coming from nowhere, came and went, feeding disturbing visions. Irritated that I could not find sleep, I sat up. However, while coming back to my senses, I realized that my attitude towards the phenomena that disturbed me had changed. Before, I would have run away from them while condemning the sky for being the culprit. Now, it was different, and I was fully aware of it. I was disappointed in myself, or rather, in my inability to control myself. "My fears are responsible… Yet again," I said, perplexed, while staring at the sacred fire a few meters from me.

I then took a few long and deep breaths to come back to my senses and refocus on myself. After about fifteen minutes, the fatigue became so unbearable that each movement, even simply turning my eyes, took a considerable amount of energy out of me. I became obsessed with the thought of lying down here on the soft sand and letting myself go until the early hours of the morning. While remembering the beautiful and peaceful death that I had experienced a few days before, I decided to lie on my comfortable yoga mat. I was aware that to fulfill the promises I made to myself at the beginning of the ceremony, I should not lie down. However, I could not fight the fatigue any longer.

Just as I closed my eyes, the voice of Hernan, the young Argentinian, abruptly brought me back:

"Brother, are you okay?" he asked with a worried tone.

As I opened my eyes with great difficulty, I saw his silhouette. He was standing, leaning over me and smiling from ear to ear, as he always does.

"Yes, yes ... brother... But it's too difficult to stay awake. I can't take it anymore," I replied while closing my eyes.

"Do you want me to help you?" he said while straightening up.

Not knowing how he planned on helping me in this seemingly hopeless situation, I reopened my eyes and answered:

"Hmm... Yes... Sure... Okay, brother..."

I then saw Hernan take a step forward and quickly grab a long and large feather amongst his ceremonial objects that he had placed in front of him before the ceremony. He then moved it quickly in front of my face. Unexpectedly, the light breeze that came from it did me a world of good. He grabbed a small bottle, then dropped a few drops of a scented solution—which reminded me of my grandfather's Cologne[1]—on my T-shirt. He also poured a few drops on the palm of his hand, which he rubbed vigorously on his over palm, then patted both my wrists. He grabbed the feather and moved it energetically several times over my hands. Finally, he burned a small piece of wood which released an extremely pleasant scent[2], brought it in front of my nostrils and swung it several times in a back-and-forth movement. As if by magic, Hernan had miraculously brought me back to life. The smells released by the burning wood and the Cologne had reached proportions that I did not know of. Strangely, it felt like they had gone straight into my soul. I pondered for a few moments during which I was amazed about the effect that ayahuasca had on each of my senses.

I sat up with the momentum of a new-found strength and thanked Hernan. I had no idea what time it was then. Looking at the sky to see the position of the moon, I realized to my dismay that it was not yet visible. I understood that the ceremony had only begun. One or two hours must have elapsed. "Oh gosh… I still need to hold on for another five or six hours," I told myself softly while sighing. As I was coming back to my senses, I remembered the promises that I had made to myself just before the ceremony: "Regardless of the difficulties that will present themselves, you cannot avoid it anymore. That means no more headphones in your ears, no more running away to the tent, no more excuses. You have to be strong." I then decided that the time that I had left had to be used positively.

Looking around me, I noticed villagers dancing around the fire. I joined them. Strangely, after a few minutes of dancing while

---

1. Which I later knew was called *Agua Florida*.

2. Which I later knew was called *Palo Santo*.

watching the vast sky above me, I realized that each step that I took around the fire filled me with happiness and gave me more energy. I then became aware of the importance of my behavior towards my own thoughts and emotions: "Afraid of being frightened, I create panic. Convinced that I'm going to collapse to the ground at any time, I generate fatigue. By forcing myself to vomit, I become certain of its absolute necessity. Fearing that I am going to have a heart attack, my chest hurts." I realized that I was the sole author of my fears and of most of my woes. At the same time, I also became aware of the paramount importance of willpower: "It is *only* through the power of my own thoughts that I am able to generate the energy and happiness I am feeling *right now*. I *alone* make my own future. I *alone* create my own experiences." Chills of happiness went through my spine. "I am the *sole author* of *my life*," I continued while treading the sand around the fire. This concept, which had not been entirely foreign to me before, had just taken a whole new dimension. Surprisingly, it had touched something inside of me that I had not been fully aware before.

From that moment until the end of the ceremony, I did not lie down. In all honesty, it was a long and difficult night. I had to fight at all times to control my thoughts and emotions and vanquish the fatigue. I told myself hundreds of times: "Do not look at the moon. Dance. Look at your steps. The time will just go by. You have no control over it. Breathe deeply. Look at your steps. Each of them is important. Move forward. Dance. Take a deep breath." When I was in the present moment, not worrying about the future or where I was, I entered a state of bliss. I dove into happiness, peace, and comfort. I knew, beyond doubt, that I was the sole author of my present.

※ ※ ※

The next day, while lying in my hammock, I thought for a long time about the ultimate aim of ayahuasca ceremonies. Amongst those thoughts, the words spoken by the famous Jaggi Vasudev Sadhguru at one of his conferences which I had the chance to attend during a stay in India came back to me. This particular talk was about the stages of the afterlife. The Indian sage stated that the quality of the passing after one dies is determined mainly by the dying person's emotions just before death. According to his explanations, the death of the physical body is immediately followed by that of the intellect. The emotional center—or function—stops after a certain amount of time, which can take up to three days[1]. Because of that, during the time the dead is deprived of the control of the intellect, the emotions created *just* before the death of the physical body is amplified exponentially to the point it becomes uncontrollable. In other words, those who are fully aware and peaceful at the time of the death of the physical body benefit from a calm passing to navigate the meanders of the afterlife, and thus, do the work needed with a view to the next incarnation. Conversely, those who die tragically, angry, drugged, in agony, or too preoccupied with their wealth, daily tasks or social status, are deprived of the capacity required to fully integrate the experiences acquired during their lifetime, thus increasing the chance of making the same mistakes during their next life.

---

1. Some philosophies mention months or years.

At that time, I thought that the Indian sage's explanations were illogical and cruel, to say the least. Indeed, why would the passing at the moment of death be determined solely by the few moments preceding it? Would the weight of an entire life not have its influence on the future of the deceased? "What an unfair mechanism!" I mentally exclaimed.

However, my most recent reflections on the past ceremonies began to make me see the question from a different angle. During my difficult challenges under the influence of ayahuasca, I noticed that each of my emotions were amplified disproportionately. In those moments, it was impossible for me to think and act logically. Even worse, when I panicked, I did so in an irreversible and uncontrollable manner. Although the explanations given to us by the Indian sage seemed absurd during the conference, they now started to make more sense. As a matter of fact, what is the real aim of the Tibetan monks if not to train themselves tirelessly to master the various states of consciousness after death, in anticipation of a better future spiritual life, and ultimately leave the infernal reincarnation cycle as described in the Bardo Thodol, *The Tibetan Book of the Dead*? Similarly, regarding ayahuasca, why would ancient shamans have given it the name of 'vine of the dead' if it was not to describe its crucial role in the training of this very discipline— mastering the stages of consciousness after death?

We all die sooner or later, whether we accept it or not. It is an inexorable and indisputable fate. Yet, in our modern societies, it must be noted that this subject is treated as if it was a contagious disease. In order to avoid the topic and live in denial, we run frantically in every direction and elaborate gigantic plans as if we were going to live for eternity. In some countries in Asia, the words that rhyme with 'death' are consciously erased from everyone's vocabulary. Very few of us are really prepared to tackle the subject matter, even fewer prepare for it. Burying our heads in the sand, however, will only work for so long.

There are countless publications that attest to the activity of consciousness after physical death, so why do we keep ignoring this subject which concerns us all? Surely, it is because our modern societies do not believe in life after death anymore. We are taught time and again that the end of physical activity *is* the end of existence as we know it. "Science has not proven that there is life after death," is the most frequent reply to silence the brave souls who dare to speak about the topic, which has become taboo in most nations. Even if some ancient religions and philosophies openly spoke about it, it is to be noted that the subject of reincarnation was mysteriously and secretly erased from most of our sacred texts only a few centuries ago.

When we go on vacation, or when we move to a new house, do we not prepare meticulously before the departure? Therefore, why do we not do the same for the most important journey that we all must go on? While incarnated, the tasks we perform, the projects which we take part in, and the responsibilities we must face have positive impact in our personal happiness, in society, or in the functioning of a nation's economy. However, all that *should not* be used as excuses to avoid the essential preparation required to positively face physical death.

❇ ❇ ❇

At the end of the day, when the sun was about to disappear, barely a few hours before the next ceremony, I concluded that even if ayahuasca was undeniably important in the preparation for physical death, it was but one aspect of it. Indeed, what is the fundamental difference of state between a man who is in a state of panic, overtaken by rage, or full of crippling emotions when facing an extraordinarily difficult situation, and a man who can control himself and remain in absolute peace? It *is* the ability to stay in the present moment. It *is* this unique quality that enables him to use all the means available to him to fully grasp a situation and make the most appropriate judgment. Similarly, what defines the quality of the passing at the moment of physical death? It *is* also the capacity to stay in the present moment that gives the dying person the tools required to positively face imminent death.

I came to the conclusion that one of ayahuasca's fundamental roles was to teach us to live in the present, and that could only be achieved if we are in total control of our thoughts and emotions.

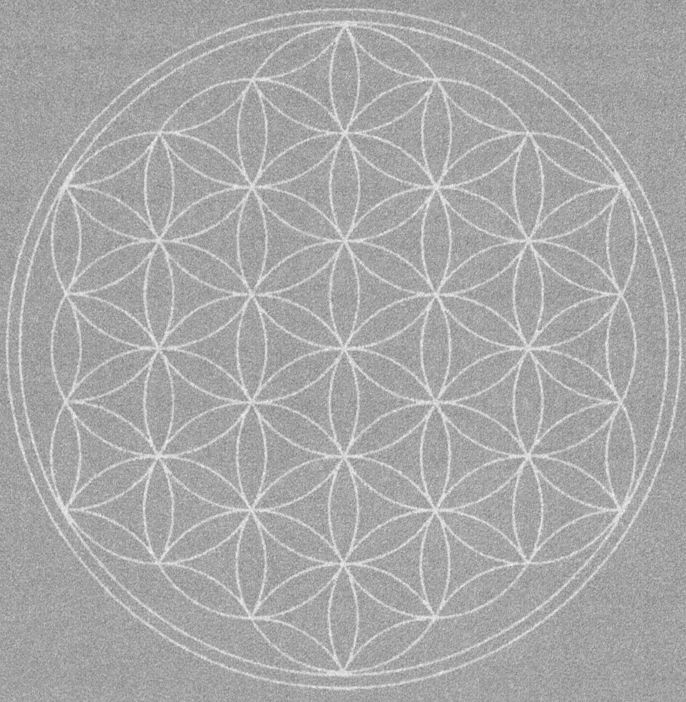

Facing Death

*When we think about how familiar death is and how total
our ignorance is, and that there has never been an escape,
we must admit that it is a well-kept secret.*
— Vladimir Jankelevitch

November 22, 2016

While preparing for the ceremony that was going to take place
that evening, I had high hopes of visiting the spiritual worlds that I
aspired to see so much. I had imagined that this would be the logical continuation of my experience with ayahuasca. At this stage of
the shamanic festival, I knew that I had obtained enough control
of my mind not to run away from the disturbing visions anymore.
However, that was not enough. I needed to gain total control of
my emotions and thoughts. I pondered deeply over how I would
achieve that state. The resulting strategy was as follows: firstly and
during the incantations, wisely alternate between sitting down with
my back straight and slowly walking around the fire. Secondly and
as soon as the music begins, take part in the snake dance, calmly
and with full awareness. Thirdly and at the right moment, meditate until my mind reaches a state of complete tranquility. Once

I had reached the desired state of mind, centered on myself, free from all random and distracting thoughts, the magic plant would open the door to the spirit world, as the late Aldous Huxley stated.

In the evening, I confidently walked towards the shamanic circle with, for the first time, confidence and head held high. Everything had been planned very carefully.

I did not imagine, however, that the ayahuasca spirit had arranged a completely different adventure for me that night.

❄ ❄ ❄

After drinking the glass that Ninawa held out to me, I sat down on a small tree trunk placed on the shamanic circle. With my back straight, I patiently waited for the first effects. As usual, they manifested themselves after about twenty minutes and caused the regular sensations. After ten more minutes, the shamanic incantations relentlessly triggered and multiplied the disturbing visions, along with their faithful hypnotic power. Despite the fatigue that started to creep in, I remained seated while focusing on my thoughts and emotions.

The chants followed, tirelessly and endlessly. At some point, the fatigue became unbearable. As it was almost impossible for me to keep my eyes open and I did not want to collapse to the ground under any circumstances, I stood up to walk a few steps. As I was standing in front of the fire, I watched the different scenes around me, one by one: the soft sand beneath my feet; the thousands of footprints left on the ground; the red and yellow colors emanating from the incandescent embers; the white smoke slowly escaping the fire and swirling towards the sky; the low and rare clouds that were sprinkled across the darkening sky; the subdued light filtered by the straw walls of the maloca; the silhouettes of the protruding, dark, and immobile shapes of the palm trees; the menacing jungle just a few steps away; the participants already sprawled out on the ground; the few brave souls who were still sitting; the majestic and frightening shamans with their tall, multicolored feather headdresses, ceremonial ornaments and tunics; the female participants with their long and jet-black hair, wearing elegant robes and adorned with scintillating jewelry which highlighted their beautiful brown skin; the motionless villagers behind the shamans; a handful of children scampering quietly around the shamanic circle; the white dog that insisted on lying down near the fire just a few moments after being chased away by the quick movements of a bamboo stick that a villager shook with enthusiasm; and the small wooden table on which the ayahuasca jar was standing with pride and detachment.

The more time passed, the more unbearable the weight of the fatigue. It was impossible for me to look at the ground without being seized with vertigo. I moved my body slowly to the rhythm of a monotonous melody that I mentally repeated to myself in order not to succumb to the hypnosis of the incantations. But the shamans seemed to be aware of what was going on in my mind. They tirelessly followed one chant with the next, non-stop. "Are they going to get the better of me this time again? Won't the night have a bit of pity for the unfortunate soul whom even the Light has abandoned?" I thought. "Be strong, stay on your feet, do not collapse," were the thoughts that started to turn into a battle which was too familiar. Was this fight against the shamans this time? Was it against my own ego? Against evil? I had no idea, but regardless of who or what my enemy were, they were dangerously gaining ground.

Then, most unexpectedly, the incantations stopped. The shamans surely needed to refresh themselves or catch their breath because despite their appearance, they were human beings too. The melody that I had been playing in my head also stopped. Just as unexpectedly, the silence became unusually heavy; the atmosphere, suffocating; the weight of the sky on my shoulders, unbearable. "Was I right to stay on my feet for all of this time? Like most of my friends, I should have perhaps saved my energy by staying seated or lying down."

Almost mechanically, I turned back and took the few steps that separated me from my seat. After a step or two, I felt unwell. Gasping for air, I rushed to sit down on the low tree trunk. I was choking. I instinctively put my hand on my chest to realize that my heart was beating very fast, too fast. From that moment on, everything accelerated: I lied down to calm my heartbeat, breathed deeply once, then again, then a third time, but to no avail. I started to panic uncontrollably. Remembering the gaze of the gentle shaman who had helped me the night before, I sat back up with great difficulty and looked for her on the outskirts. She was not there. Nobody was there. None of my friends were conscious. From what I could see, only the person who was taking care of the fire was awake. It was Tao. He was crouching and stirring the embers with a long stick. While crawling on the sand, I crossed the few meters that separated us.

"What's wrong, Adriano?" Tao asked me while turning towards me.

"Tao, I'm not well. I'm not feeling well at all. My heart is beating too quickly. Please get a doctor."

"No, no, Adriano. Don't panic. Go back to your seat and take deep breaths. You'll quickly feel better," he replied while smiling broadly.

"Damn… He doesn't understand. He doesn't understand what's happening to me at all. I'm done," I thought, very alarmed.

"Go back to your seat, Adriano, and breathe deeply," Tao added with a grin on his face.

With a great deal of effort, I dragged myself backwards until I reached my seat. Lying on my yoga mat, I was exhausted and short-winded. My heart was in my throat and was hurting terribly. The accumulation of night-long ceremonies, the torrid heat and excessive humidity of the Amazon jungle, the itches caused by the countless insect bites that refused to heal, the banana-based dishes that made me nauseous just thinking about them, my countless musings and theories that collapsed one after the other like a house of cards, my constant torments, unanswered questions, and unfulfilled dreams, had worn me out. Also, as the festival was ending, I realized that I would never know why I had come here, in the middle of the ruthless Amazon forest. Was it all worth it in the end?

At that point, my quest for spirituality and answers to my existential questions had become absurd. I was tired of this senseless life. My battles had lost their reason to exist. I did not want to carry on like this. I let my arms fall flat along my body and stopped worrying about my racing heart and my desperate situation. I also stopped worrying about my fate. After a few long and deep breaths, some-how, I was in peace. I intuitively knew that I was about to die, but I was calm at that thought. Ayahuasca had taken me so close and so often to the jaws of death that this situation was now familiar. "Also, what good would fighting do? What could justify another battle?" I knew that my time had come. It was inevitable, it was my exit. I knew that I would slip to the other side as soon as my heart stopped beating. I smiled at the thought that although *my* heart was a part of *my* own body, of *my* being, of *me*, it was it that was to decide of *my* fate, and I had no say in it.

Unlike the previous ceremonies in which colored visions paraded in front of my eyes when my eyelids closed, everything was now dark, pitch dark. No colors. No shapes. No celestial dances. A dark shadow had invaded the entire horizon after consuming all the light along the way. Only the pervasive and almost unbearable noise of my heartbeats and the back-and-forth sound of my deep and endless breaths were keeping me alive.

The terrible incantations had stopped. My friends had also left me. I could not feel my body anymore. My breathing was barely audible. After a long and endless exhalation, it too finally stopped. The final beat of my loyal companion followed, causing a strangely muffled and stifled explosion. I was surprised to still be conscious to notice it. I had always thought that the conscience left the body shortly before or exactly at the moment of physical death. Then, nothing. No sound, no feeling. I knew that I wasn't anymore. I was no longer part of this world that had made me suffer so much. I was no longer part of this world that had been so unfair to me and to those whom I had loved tenderly. There was nothing but total darkness around me. Then, nothing, for an indescribably long time.

I must have lost consciousness afterwards. All I remember are the times when I regained consciousness with a long, endless, and painful inhalation through my constricted throat while mentally exclaiming: "Oh gosh... I am still here... I am not dead yet... How is this possible? How much longer..." Each time, it was unspeakable agony. At that time, knowing whether there was an afterlife or not was the least of my worries. None of that mattered anymore. I wanted the torture to end. Each time, the breathing continued for a few moments, weakened, then stopped again in the same endless nightmare.

Finally, it went dark. Then, nothing.

❄ ❄ ❄

When I recovered my senses, a voice far away repeated with a worried tone:

"Brother... Are you okay? Do you need help? Are you okay? Brother... Do you need help?"

It was Hernan. With a lot of difficulty and a lump in my throat, I answered:

"Yes... No... No..."

"Do you need help, is that it? Okay, what can I do?"

"Doctor... Go... Get... Doctor... Go... Doctor..."

"What? Do you want me to go and get the doctor?"

"Yes…"

"Oh… Okay," Hernan replied while standing up. Just before he left, he took off the wool shawl that he had wrapped around himself and put it on me. I immediately felt comforted and warm. After the long blackout, it was the first time that I could feel my body again. Then, once again, it was complete darkness.

I regained consciousness when I felt that my head was being lifted by two hands placed behind my skull. Through my barely open eyelids I saw the silhouette of a shaman wearing an animal skin tunic. His powerful forearms were covered by brightly colored geometric patterns. I saw the tip of the feathers of his tall headdress coming and going in front of my face. While tipping my head from right to left, he strongly blew tobacco smoke on the top of my skull. The smell and the smoke were unbearable. I could not breathe. He then massaged my temples, hands, and forearms, breathed tobacco smoke several times into each ear, on the chests, pressed the top of my head with force, lifted my torso and moved it from right to left, then back to front. Nothing could make me regain consciousness for more than a few instants. I felt like a powerless spectator, barely conscious and trapped in a body over which I had no control. "Oh… He is trying to revive me…" I silently muttered. "Please continue… Do not stop… Please…" I continued. Each touch of his strong and agile hands resonated in me like as he was hitting a heavy drum. Although his powerful puffs of tobacco smoke gave me the impression that they were traversing my body from one end to the other, they were incapable of reaching or reviving my soul. I begged the mysterious shaman to never stop, but my thoughts were too weak; I felt the cold sand below my head. I was alone and abandoned, once again. Then, nothing.

When I woke up, I saw Ninawa's face. He was in front of me with his majestic headdress. It was the most beautiful and imposing of all the headdresses I had seen. The chief shaman appeared to be still. The sound space was now made of two distinct chants; that of the shamans in the distance, and Ninawa's. He was singing for me. His powerful and calm voice was familiar and comforting to my ears. With a strength and power that are unknown in our normal reality, his incantations were directly addressing my soul. I felt it. I felt as if my mind, my ego, was silent and docile, perhaps for the very first time. The chief shaman was probably summoning the angels from the sky for my salvation. Was it a dream? Was it the end? Was I finally going to leave? Then, again, nothing. Ninawa, with his majestic headdress and flamboyant body paintings, disappeared as mysteriously as he had appeared.

Every time I regained consciousness, I had the faint impression that I had come from afar. These moments, the first sensation of the outside world that I would experience was the shamanic incantations. They filled the entire space. Their all-pervasiveness and omnipotence seemed to organize time and space. The incantations orchestrated the rare moments I was awake and governed those I had lost consciousness. I could not comprehend why they lasted so long. Where did the shamans obtain their superhuman energy from? It was beyond understanding.

As odd as it may sound, it is only then that I became fully aware of the vast superiority of the forces behind my experience that night. They were manifestly far greater than my own. I always considered myself to be someone who was mentally strong. I believed that my intensive training in several martial arts and yoga had prepared me well for any test. However, how could it be conceivable to find myself drifting uncontrollably between the shores of life and death? What happened to me? Who allowed such a fate, such torture, such humiliation? Why did my ego not save me as it always does, callously and with no pity for who I really am? Contrary to the previous ceremonies, in which I managed to keep a certain amount of control over my physical capacities and, to a certain extent, my mental capacities, that was not the case on this night. I found myself there, intermittently conscious, lying on the ground with my head in the sand. Also, when I realized that I was being watched by my friends during all this agony, I felt ashamed. "What are they thinking? How are they judging me?" This new reality was difficult to bear. "At the end of the day, who am I, really? Why do I deserve this sordid fate? Am I an evil soul of some sort?"

When I reopened my eyes, I noticed the silhouette of a few of the participants who were sitting around the fire. My reduced field of vision prevented me from seeing the entire circle. The glow of the fire that emanated from between my friends invited me to join them. Crawling on the sand, I managed to sit between two participants. Immediately after finding a more or less comfortable position, I felt so nauseous that I let out a succession of burps that I could not control. I felt that the 'beast' that had grown inside my entrails now wanted to leave. Each burp amplified my embarrassment towards my friends who were physically so close. An irresistible fatigue took hold of me. I lowered my head, then nothing. I lost consciousness once again.

Every time I opened my eyes, the setting was different. At one moment I was lost in a dark and deep jungle. Another moment I was lying near the fire, then near a swamp, or on the outskirts of a wooden cabin. How did I end up there? Did I move myself? Did someone move me without my realizing it? I had no idea.

Nausea made me regain consciousness several times, but the vile liquid and the monstrous reptile stubbornly refused to leave my entrails. Only the sounds of my uncontrollable burps filled the space. They seemed so loud to me that I thought they came from elsewhere. "How can I make such appalling noises..." I thought with horror.

After a long time, I opened my eyes and looked around me. Apart from the weak glow that emanated from the fire, everything was dark. I then had the idea to reach the shamans to ask for help. My thinking was to walk along the periphery of the circle formed by the participants, which would lead me to the shamans one way or another. With an almost superhuman effort, I sat down, then stood up. From where I was and for some reason, I could not see the shamans in real—in a flow of images—but as an odd mixture of sounds and blurry flashes. Their incantations formed an array of lines of different colors that seemed to emanate from them. Staggering and in a clumsy way, I followed the 'bright sounds'. When I was probably only a few meters away from the source, the intensity of the incantations became unbearable. The shamans seemed to be shouting directly into my ears. Each syllable bombarded my soul to the point that I was unable to take another step. Dragging my feet, I took a detour behind the furious horde. Exhausted, I continued my path along the circle to collapse on the sand a few steps away. Then, nothing. There was total darkness for a long time.

When I came back to my senses, I felt nauseous. After straightening up, I sat on my heels, leaned forward, tried to vomit, but in vain. Only the horrible and endless burps escaped. On the sand in front of me, I saw the shadow of my body projected by the glow of the fire. I noticed that it was not outlining the body that I was accustomed to, but that of a dragon. Large and pointy scales adorned its outline. A kind of spike-shaped crest formed the top of my skull. At one moment, I saw myself from above as if I was hovering over my body; the next moment, I had changed perspective and found myself in my body, facing the shadow projected on the sand. I intuitively knew that I was a young dragon, still in its infancy.

Every time I woke up, the discomfort regarding my state of weakness in front of my friends tortured me. However, and quite curiously, at this point of the ceremony the feeling of shame and embarrassment started to take a different turn. I became aware that something in my personality had changed. I then rejoiced at the idea that, maybe, I was becoming the person I had wanted to be for a long time: a loving and authentic person, someone who is liberated from fear and ego, someone whole. This thought warmed my heart. Also, unlike the previous ceremonies, I realized that I had not been taken over by fear, I had not accused the shamans of being part of an evil or satanic act, I had neither fought ferociously nor escaped as I had done many times before. This time, there was no fight against my imaginary demons or myself. There were no horrible monsters, no harmful entities, no visions, and no multicolored lights. There was only me. None other than my own self.

With the inexorable certitude that the person I had been was dying, I curled into the fetal position on the sand. In blissful peace, I took a deep breath in, followed by a long exhalation. I intuitively knew that everything was as it should be.

My eyelids closed themselves. Then, once again, nothing.

❄ ❄ ❄

The warmth of a hand placed on my shoulder made me regain consciousness. I was still in the same position. I did not know how long I had been curled up on the sand for. I could neither move nor open my eyes but, by intuition, I knew that the hand belonged to a woman whom I saw during the second ceremony, the woman whom I nicknamed 'Avatar,' as her eyes were so wide and beautiful. Curiously, I saw her place her hand on my shoulder as if an observer had captured the scene during my absence and was now projecting it on my closed eyes. I could now observe her intention, her gaze, and her bright face, almost in slow motion. I watched the scene from the inside of my body as if it was transparent. From there, I saw my friend put her hand on my shoulder. Then, pitch black, once again.

When I briefly regained consciousness, I heard a voice say: "He is stuck between two worlds." Who was it? I never found out.

When I opened my eyes again, a small bottle containing water had been placed in front of me, about thirty centimeters away from my face. As it had been the case for 'Avatar,' I knew who had put the bottle there. It was Ian. I barely knew him until that point. We had crossed paths several times before, but we had never exchanged more than a few words. He was now sitting a meter to my right.

He was looking in front of him, in the direction of the fire, while watching over me. "Oh… Water…" I told myself before passing out once more. When I reopened my eyes, Ian had moved the bottle further towards me. It was now about ten centimeters away, just in front of my forehead. I did not understand how he could envisage letting me drink directly from his bottle knowing that I was so dirty after rolling in the sand all night, trying to vomit, alternating between man and dragon. His gesture and compassion towards me touched me deeply. I lost consciousness several times after that. Every time I reopened my eyes, the bottle and its owner were there, by my side. I found it curious that the small bottle was so significant to my friend. Did it have a role to play in my recovery? I had to find out.

I then gathered enough strength to grab the bottle and bring it to my mouth. While doing so, it felt like I had not moved a muscle in an eternity. Although every centimeter demanded a considerable amount of effort, it made me joyful, for I was under the impression that I was escaping the world of the dead to get closer to that of the living. After tilting the bottle enough for a few drops of water to flow from its valve, I took a first sip, followed by a second, and a third. I then saw the water travel from the inside of my body as an extraordinarily bright blue light. I observed it go through my mouth, throat, esophagus, and finally, my stomach. It then illuminated my lungs, heart, as well as all of my organs, one by one, as if it had a strong regenerative power. I then took a long and deep breath, which pushed the energy further into the deepest parts of my physical body.

I let my head rest on the sand, then took a few deep breaths. I had the ineffable sensation that I had come from afar, that I had come back from the dead. I was now feeling full of life, probably for the very first time. I lost consciousness several times after that, but each time I recovered my senses, Ian put his hand on my shoulder and said: "It will be fine brother, it will be fine." Having had such a comforting presence at my side in these moments of agony in which I felt the most vulnerable and lost was the most precious thing of all. It is in these moments that I became fully aware of the importance of compassion. The frantic hunt for material possessions that takes so much importance in our societies, which to some extent can be justified in the survival of our species, will never bring us the vital element for self-realization: unconditional love. The suffering that reigns and cripples our planet is undeniably the result of the lack of this very quality, of this divine energy.

When I looked up again, I saw Ian. He was sitting on the sand with his back straight. His position reminded me of the importance of keeping that posture during ayahuasca ceremonies. With a superhuman effort, I sat up to do the same. Although I was unable to keep my back straight for more than a few instants, I was happy to be sitting for the first time in what seemed like an eternity. Seeing me in this position, Ian exclaimed with a broad smile while raising his hand to the sky: "Welcome back, brother!" He quickly stood up, then sat down just next to me, to my right, putting his arm around my shoulder. The young woman whom I had nicknamed 'Avatar' sat to my left and took my hand. I looked at them in turn, then with a big smile, I said: "Thank you. Thank you both. Thank you, brother. I felt your presence at all times. You were there. It is thanks to you that I have come back to life. It is thanks to both of you. Thank you with all of my heart." I was unable to utter any more words, but my eyes must surely have been saying much more. After a few moments, Avatar shed a few tears, then stood up to meet her friends by the fire. Ian stayed.

His enthusiasm made me want to try to straighten my back again. After several attempts, I eventually sat down in the yogi position, with my legs crossed in half-lotus and my back somehow straight. This process required a lot of effort. I was panting and exhausted, but very happy.

Then, I started to remember the events of the night, one after the other, in slow motion. One moment, I saw them through my eyes, then from outside of me, a meter or two above my shoulders. I could not believe that all that had really happened. Yet, the scenes were vivid and real. I watched them without judging. I was in peace, fulfilled, and taken over by sheer happiness. The feeling of the soft sand beneath my palms was unusually pleasant; perhaps was I really touching sand for the first time? The air that entered through my nostrils was light and fragrant; perhaps was I really breathing for the first time? The light was comforting to my eyes and heart; perhaps was I really contemplating light for the first time? One thing was certain, however, I felt really alive for the first time.

I heard music notes, playing one after the other, like floating in the air. They did not appear to be connected to create a whole. My mind was unable to assemble them into a melody. However, I was surprised to notice that the shamanic songs had finally ended. The villagers, as well as a few of my friends, were around the fire. They seemed to be moving in slow motion. I understood that they were dancing. I wanted to join them. I needed to feel my body move to the rhythm of the music. However, standing up, walking, and dancing were concepts that I was still unable to explore, even mentally. I watched the dancers wiggle slowly around the fire for a long time. The musical notes were also there. Under the weight of the fatigue, I lost consciousness several times. At one point, I saw Ian standing up and walking to the other side of the shamanic circle. I told myself that I could not fall asleep again, or else my chances of joining the dancers would vanish. With the help of my hands on the sand, I lifted a leg, then the other, and finally stood up. Despite a constant struggle to keep balance, I was finally on my feet. "You will not lie down again. You will not sit down, until sunrise," I solemnly said to myself while staring at the sand in front of my feet.

I started to move my body by making barely discernible movements. I then became aware that I was still wearing the wool shawl that Hernan had put on me before looking for help. I watched it hanging from both shoulders, which made me think of a cape. I felt like a caveman covered in sand and dust, coming back from a long and perilous journey.

I trampled on the sand around the fire for a long time, a very long time. My movements improved progressively as my brain managed to connect the musical notes to make a melody and regain control over my muscles. As I had sworn to myself, I danced until sunrise without fail. Several times, I was taken over by an irresistible urge to fall to the ground and close my tired eyes, but in order not to give in to the temptation, I looked at the sky above, took a deep breath through my nose, followed by a slow exhalation from the mouth, then continued to dance tirelessly, one step after the other, with a constant presence. There were no past and no future, no questions and no comments, no worries and no thoughts. Only the present mattered.

✳ ✳ ✳

After a long time, I looked around me and decided to go back to my initial seat. Curiously, after a few minutes had passed, the air became extremely heavy. There was no life on the outskirts of the circle. Most of my friends were motionless, either still sprawled on the ground or sitting on the sand. Many of them had a blank look. Some whispered amongst themselves, others moved slowly, all in total silence.

Then, as if a lead blanket weighing me down, each of the night's events began to pass before my eyes: the agony while facing death, the desperate search for a doctor, the shaman's efforts to revive me, Ninawa's incantations, the moments when I was seemingly life-less, my face in the cold sand, the constant urge to vomit, the end-less burps, the shadow of the dragon on the sand, Avatar, Ian, and the feeling of discomfort towards my friends. Strangely, instead of rejoicing in the experience that I had just been through, I felt humiliated for having lost my composure in front of my friends. I felt ashamed that they had watched all my struggles. This feeling gradually became overwhelming. I felt naked. "How am I going to act in front of them tomorrow? What are they going to think of me? What am I going to say to them?" While looking at the sand beneath my feet, I remained lost in my thoughts for a long time.

The Sun finally appeared. Some of the participants stood up to hug each other. I joined them. I needed that. They asked me if I was feeling better now. With a half-smile, I answered that I was. I lied. I felt humiliated, empty, dirty, heavy, and lacking energy. Some of the participants underlined that I had spent a large part of the night lying down near the fire with my head in the sand and that the dancers had to be careful not to step on me. Others told me that it happened to everyone at some point or another. Others said that I would be stronger after this experience. I smiled and kept quiet because I did not know how to answer. What could I say? I would have liked to not exist anymore, to fly away. I would have liked for the night to take me away, as it should have.

I saw Ninawa hugging some of the participants, notably those who were normally close to him. I crossed the few meters that separated us, looked into his eyes, and gestured that I also wanted a hug. Surprised, he smiled at me, opened his arms, and gave me a long, friendly hug. I thanked him for the evening. Although we did not speak the same language, his eyes told me that he had understood. His friendship and almost superhuman strength and presence did me a world of good.

The chief shaman then called all the participants to gather around the fire to say a prayer. Side by side, we repeated Ninawa's words. Although my emotions did not give me any respite, the sky outside was clear, sunny, and bright, as it should be.

I left the circle afterwards to make my way to my hut. I opened my tent's zipper just enough to slide inside and lay down on the plastic mattress, then placed my head on the deflated pillow. My eyelids closed.

That morning, I found sleep without difficulty.

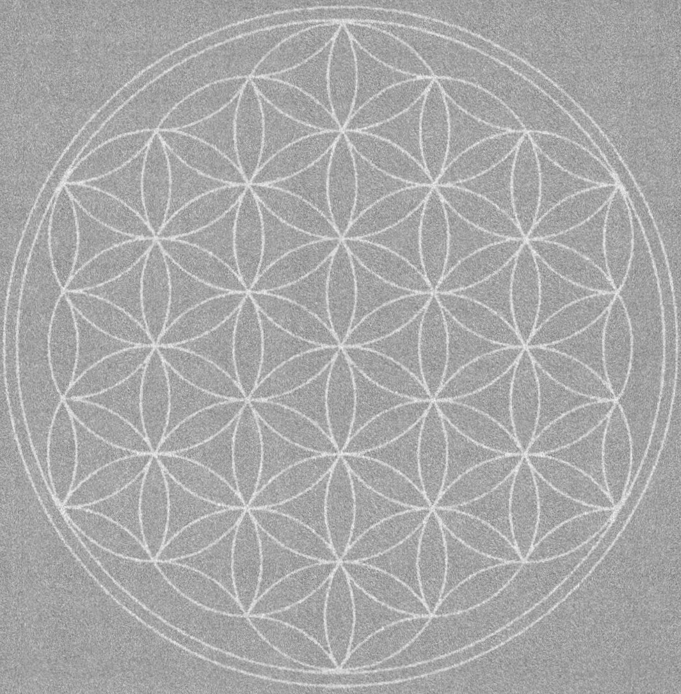

Spiritual Autonomy

The life of man depends on his will;
without will, it would be left to chance.
— Confucius

November 26, 2016 — four days after the ceremony facing death

As I was reading over my notes describing the day that followed the last ceremony, I struggled to believe what I had written in my small notebook. I found it particularly difficult to realize the strong emotions I experienced that particular day. It was unlike me. Apart from the occasional anger resulting from my impatience towards life or the goals I had set for myself and not yet achieved, my unyielding intellect had always made sure I stay in control of my emotions.

At first, I decided not to share or speak about the contents of these notes with my friends. On the one hand, I saw the notes as a little too personal, and on the other hand, I believed they were not particularly significant in my experience with ayahuasca. It is only after I was able to think more rationally I realized that, although emotionally exhausting, the day that followed the ceremony when I faced death had a significant importance in my learning with shamanism and ayahuasca as well as in my spiritual development.

Before I share my experience, however, I do need to add that one of the characteristics of ayahuasca is that it significantly amplifies the emotions of those who consume it. A person prone to sadness will feel unlimited sorrow under the effects of this ruthless decoction; the one consumed by anger will accuse and condemn the whole universe for their shortcomings; those who sincerely seek peace will sail on the waters of a perfectly calm sea; a person who genuinely looks for divinity will bathe in a divine light that is unseen in our dimensions. Under the effects of ayahuasca, nothing is hidden; every minute detail of a person's character is exposed to oneself, and often, for all to see.

❄ ❄ ❄

November 23, 2016 — the day after the ceremony facing death

When I woke up, the Sun was already high in the sky. It was hot and humid. The memories of the ceremony from the night before started to haunt me. I could not comprehend why I had had to go through such agony. I could not accept that I had lost control of my physical and mental capacities to that extent. Above all, I was tormented with embarrassment caused by the fact that it had taken place in front of my friends. My pride had been shattered along with my self-confidence. Still lying in my hammock, I was crippled by the thought of seeing my friends again. After being lost in my thoughts for quite some time, I came to terms that I would have to face reality sooner or later. I concluded that the sooner I confronted what was tormenting me, the sooner I would be freed from it.

Outside of the hut, the air was fresh. The canteen was empty. The dishes had also been emptied. The crumbs on the table indicated that I had missed breakfast. I walked to the large jug and served myself a coffee in a plastic cup. Two sugars. The coffee was barely warm. I sat at one of the long empty tables. It was one of the first times, if not the first time, that there was total silence. There was no sign of life on the outskirts of the canteen, neither in the large space where the ceremonies had taken place, nor in front of the maloca. I drank my coffee while thinking about the night before, once again.

When I returned to the hut, I saw Aesha sitting on the small wooden bench along the window. She did not take part in the ceremony the night before, because she felt that she needed to rest. "Oh... She was right to listen to herself!" I thought, "Why didn't I do the same..." While conversing with Aesha, I learned that the ceremony was particularly difficult for the majority of us. The main reason was the prolonged length of the shamanic chants. According to my friend, the shamans uttered their incantations until four o'clock in the morning, which was far longer than the previous ceremonies. "How is Yogesh?" I asked her, concerned that I had not seen him yet. She nodded while biting her lip. "Oh ... but he is fine, right?" I added. "Well... Yes... He'll be fine... He is resting in the tent."

Aesha shared nightmares she had until late in the night. The description was so vivid that it sent shivers down my spine. She then asked me how I was feeling. After I answered briefly, her face saddened, as if she had rightly intercepted my emotions. As my heart was heavy and I needed to share my burden with someone, anyone, I began to tell her what happened during the ceremony. While carefully listening to each word, her eyes were wide open, stuck in an expression of amazement. Curiously, although I promised myself not to talk about this subject with anyone barely an hour before, I hid nothing from Aesha. My reticence quickly faded under her compassionate gaze. I felt safe and in peace during this genuine exchange. It was a rare opportunity to find this type of relationship. Strangely, as I was relating the events of the ceremony to Aesha, I started to see them differently; I was under the impression that the seriousness and weight I had given them was progressively fading away. We conversed for over an hour. That afternoon, Aesha's tenderness, attentiveness, compassion, and smiles appeased my soul more than she could ever imagine.

The hours following that conversation were difficult. I felt that I was drunk, like a robot receiving distant images in slow motion through a fuzzy pane of scratched glass. My gait was unsteady. It was unbearably hot and oppressively humid. I took a shower, but the mosquitoes came at me as if from a fire hose. A wave of thoughts and doubts identical to those from the morning haunted me constantly. "Why have I lived this miserable experience? Did I really deserve that? Have I lost forever the person I was? I know that I am not a bad person per se, so why such treatment, such torture, such agony? Could it be that ayahuasca is *just* another drug, no more, no less, that has now inflicted incurable damage on me?" I was firmly convinced that I had irreparably ruined my soul.

While leaving the shower, I noticed a few people gathered in front of the canteen. It was lunch time. When I entered the hut, I saw that about ten people were sitting around one of the long wooden tables. I served myself some food, then sat at the only empty table. I was not ready to face my friends' stares and questions yet. One of the participants walked into the hut and sat beside me. After exchanging smiles, he told me that he saw me last night.

"Oh my! You were struggling... Your head was in the sand and everything!" he exclaimed while laughing.

"Yes, right. It wasn't an easy night," I answered.

I turned my head towards my dish. A few moments later, Scott came in and sat to my right. He smiled at me. I knew his kindness, precious advice, and attentiveness, which was comparable to that of Aesha, Asil, and Rory. He asked me if I was well, and I broadly told him last night's events. He listened to every detail carefully. Then, I asked him:

"Has that already happened to you, Scott?"

"Yes, more than once... But you will see, Adriano, you will quickly feel better. It is a path that a lot of us must go on. You will see, do not worry about it, you will soon feel better."

"Yes... I suppose. Tell me, why must we go through this? Are humans that evil deep down?"

"I don't think so. I consider this experience to be an opportunity to face our inner demons. As a result, we create the tools needed to grow spiritually."

"Is there no other way? I mean, a *less* extreme way?"

"I don't really know. It seems that we do need to cross these dark tunnels to manifest the light in us."

"What have we done as humans to deserve such a fate?"

I knew that there wasn't an easy answer to that, so I quickly followed with the next question.

"Scott, when will that feeling of being lost… I mean … of having lost your soul, stop? Hmm… When will I know that I have become someone else? I mean… When will I receive confirmation that the process is complete… That it has been successful?"

My question was muddled. I was confused. I could not clearly formulate the question that was consuming me so much. I wanted to know *when* the nightmare in which I felt imprisoned would finally end. I also wanted to know if I had made an irreparable mistake taking part in yesterday's ceremony, or consuming ayahuasca. Scott looked up and stared at the canteen straw ceiling. After a few moments, I could tell from his expression that he had understood my *real* question. He then replied:

"Well, when *you* decide, Adriano."

In a very curious way, those words struck a chord in me, so much so that I instinctively knew they were going to be important to me in the near future. Scott's intuition had remarkably calmed my soul. My heart was finally starting to heal. Like Aesha, Asil, and Rory, I am indebted to Scott for the time that he spent relieving the heart of a stranger in distress.

The organizers asked us to gather in front of the canteen to take part in a ceremony of sacred baths organized by the shamans and villagers. After walking for about twenty minutes through the dense forest, we arrived in front of the gigantic Samaúma, a sacred tree located by a shallow stream. The men of the village were sitting on one of its enormous roots. Some of the villagers were playing guitar, others were singing, and others were smoking Peruvian tobacco. The women, sitting a few steps away, were either doing their hair, applying makeup, humming, or singing. Others were seating further along the tree trunks laid on the ground.

A small group of older women, probably around sixty or seventy years of age, were filling large buckets of water. Flowers and herbs were floating on the surface. The organizers asked us to undress to our swimming suit, short or underwear. In turn, we were to stand, in front of the village's female shamans to receive a sacred bath. I recognized the shaman who made me aware of my fears during a previous ceremony. While walking towards her, I smiled. Returning my smile, she gestured to move closer to her. I was surprised by how white her teeth were. Her tender appearance, infinite compassion, and cheerful and bright eyes warmed my heart. We were a few steps away from the limpid stream, close to the sacred tree. The countless types of plants, trees and vines made the setting surreal. The foliage above was so dense that it was nearly impossible to see the sky. The noise of the streaming water soothed me. It was cooler in the forest than in the village. The shaman told me to lower myself to receive the bath, which I did promptly by putting one knee on the ground. She then grabbed the bucket in which a few petals and leaves were floating, then lifted it with surprising ease, and poured a part of its contents on my shoulders. The lukewarm water sliding down my body created a blissful feeling. With the help of a branch with leaves, she rubbed my body with a slow back-and-forth movement while quietly uttering harmonic incantations. So much wisdom and compassion emanated from the mysterious white-haired angel woman that it seemed she had repeated the same movements for millennia. She then poured the rest of the water on the top of my head to rinse me. The soft fragrance of the plants, flowers, and essential oil mixture was almost supernatural. I wanted it to never end. I thanked the shaman, to which she gave me a tender smile.

Once sitting on one of the neighboring tree trunks, the harsh reality of the jungle abruptly brought me back; a swarm of mosquitoes had surrounded me and was beginning to attack. Still wet, I jumped into my clothes and quickly walked to the hut where I could retreat in my mosquito net and lie safely in my hammock.

On the way I met Yogesh. He told me that Bernard was feeling unwell. "He is stuck between two worlds," he added. I promised that I would see him immediately. When I entered the hut where Bernard was, I saw him lying on the floor. Three female shamans and two of my friends were watching over him. Lying on the wooden floor, he squirmed slowly while articulating sounds that I could not understand, as if he wanted to get out of something that was keeping him prisoner. One of the shamans raised Bernard's head to make him drink a whitish potion in a small ceramic bowl. Another blew tobacco smoke on his torso while shaking a branch with leaves along his body, from head to toes. I asked one of my friends about Bernard's condition with a look, to which she answered with a discrete shake of the head indicating he was not fine.

The heat and humidity in this part of the jungle were unusual for this time of the year. Unable to do anything for my friend, I exited the hut and returned to mine to rest. Once in my hammock, I thought that I would quickly fall asleep. It could not have been further from the truth. Despite my exhaustion, the scenes of the night before and of the other ceremonies appeared on a loop behind my closed eyelids. The more I tried to control them, the more relentless they became. All my thoughts were amplified to such proportions that they were draining all my energy. The heat was unbearable. I was sweating profusely. I was convinced that I was suffocating. At one point, my thoughts led be to believe that my heart was beating too quickly, but my hand placed on it confirmed it was beating normally. "What if it was beating too slowly because I am too tired? That's it… it's going to stop!" I mentally exclaimed. Priscilla and Hernan were in the room next door. I called for help, but the sounds that came out of my throat were too weak to reach them. I struggled to even hear them myself. I tried several times, but the result was invariably the same. "They surely are sleeping." I concluded, "How lucky…"

After some time, Priscilla walked by my hammock. While exchanging a few words, she advised me to follow her to the hut where Bernard was. When we arrived, I tapped my friend's shoulder, then lied in the circle that three female shamans, Priscilla, and two other women had formed. I recognized the shaman with the beautiful smile and angelic hair. As soon as I lied on the floor, she looked at one of my friends and told her that I was not well. "He is not feeling well. He is not going to die, but he is not feeling well," She said. Simply being in the same space as this woman made me feel better. I felt more in peace. After a few moments, she gestured for me to sit up. While quietly uttering harmonious incantations, she blew tobacco smoke into my ears, nostrils, and the top of my skull, then massaged my head, torso, arms, and head. The shaman then turned to my friend to continue treating him.

Immediately after standing up, I felt very nauseous. I burped a few times. "Keep your mouth shut this time…" I told myself while smiling and thinking about the night before. While looking at my friend, the shaman told her with a grin that 'it' was coming out. I took a few steps outside of the hut, then vomited a very acidic liquid. I felt a sense of freshness. My thoughts became clearer. The intoxication faded.

I returned to the hut to thank the shaman and discretely asked Priscilla if I should offer something to the shaman for the treatment that she had so graciously given me. She told me that giving money was not custom here, but a gift would certainly be welcome. I asked her what kind of gift would be acceptable, to which she replied that it did not matter. Considering everything that this woman had done for me, I promised that I would give her my tent before I left. She gave me a big grin because this kind of item was quite welcomed in the jungle, whether it be to protect resting children from insects or to temporarily store supplies for the same reason.

While exiting the hut, I helped Sylvie walk to the canteen. The day before, she inadvertently stepped on a stingray while bathing in the river with the children of the village. It was so painful that the village doctor had to inject her with morphine[1]. Although she was still unable to put her foot on the ground, she was looking better.

---

1. I was told it was morphine by another friend, but it could have been something else.

We had been in the depths of the forest for close to three weeks, and it was starting to weigh on each and everyone of us. Even the very few who had not been affected physically or mentally by the extreme conditions of the jungle were exhausted. We moved and walked in slow motion. We were all absorbed by our thoughts and emotions. The atmosphere was morose and smiles had become rare.

Personally, and especially on that day, all my sensations, emotions, and each moment were very amplified and disproportionate. I felt that I was connected to the trees, the plants, the animals, and to my peers. Odors were piercing. Food had taste again. Colors were brighter than ever. I felt as if my skin was vibrating in harmony with its environment. For the first time, my entire being seemed to be part of a whole.

Looking back, while writing these lines in a little Himalayan tea room in Western China a few months later, I am smiling. However, in the jungle, everything was real. I did not know if it was the case for my friends, but for me, each of these moments was lived as if thousands of emotions were brawling in me, each more intense than the last. It was both magical and difficult. One moment I felt intensely happy for no logical reason, the next I was crippled by panic for a motive that did not make sense, the minute after I was saying my goodbyes to life because I was convinced that it was going to escape my body at once, then I was at peace, or demanding my emotions to be even more intense because I felt more alive than I had ever been.

When we arrived at the canteen, Sylvie and I sat around one of long wooden tables. I happened to sit next to Ian, the friend who watched over me during a large part of the previous ceremony. I tapped his shoulder and asked him how he was feeling. Without really looking at me, he slid along the bench and moved half a meter away. Jorge was shelling nuts. I spoke to him, but he ignored me. I then tried to start a conversation with Veronica, who was sitting across me, but she looked at me with what appeared to be disdain and looked away. No one was speaking. I felt that everyone had become quiet when I entered the canteen. I felt as if I had become invisible.

From then on, it all escalated in my mind; I became overtaken by paranoia. "No one is speaking to me anymore. They are no longer looking at me. Why are they ignoring me? What have I become? What do I look like right now? Am I *that* horrible? Why did I attend the ceremony yesterday? I was doing just fine before that…" These questions followed and intensified in my mind. I felt as if I had no control over anything anymore. Just as I did upon waking up that morning, I dwelled on the utility of the last ceremony and on my life on Earth. I felt like I was a pariah, a drunkard, a social reject. "Gosh… It's probably what beggars feel most of the time," I thought, when I had a moment of clarity, before sinking back into distress. The idea that my friends might also have had trouble with the past ceremony did not even occur to me. I felt lonely and misunderstood. No one was there to reassure me. Neither a smile nor a look. It suddenly felt cold in the ruthless jungle.

Looking at the canteen's entrance, which was only a few steps away, I stood up and walked towards it. "No one looked at me. No one even noticed that I have left. They must have breathed a sigh of relief upon seeing me leave," I thought while walking away. Like a robot, I headed to my hut to grab my towel and soap. I needed a bath. Once I had taken my clothes off in the small doorless and roofless wooden shower cabin, I opened the tap to let water slide on my body. While looking at the sky above, I silently uttered: "God, why have you done this to me? Why have you left me alone? Why such suffering?" I asked the same questions over and over. To appease my soul, I desperately needed to shed tears, but my body was too dry and exhausted.

Sighing deeply while looking at the sky, I questioned: "When will all of this *stop*?"

At that moment, although I had reached the deepest abyss and touched the darkest place in my soul, a voice broke the silence and said: "It is you that has the key. You, and *only* you can heal yourself." The exchange that I had with Scott that morning echoed in my ears. His words now made complete sense. They resonated powerfully in me. "You, and *only* you have the power to rise from your ashes," added the deep voice. I then felt an intense light from inside of me. It was more real and powerful than anything that I had ever felt. Those words had, somehow, touched my soul.

I remained a long time under the lukewarm water heated by the Amazon sunrays. I slowed time to wash each fragment of my soul. I saw all my past experiences, the most beautiful as well as the most painful ones. Everything began to make sense. All my struggles and exertions were justified. I had the feeling that the equation that had governed my life and that I had accused of so much injustice could now be solved. I did not know how yet, or which path to take, but I had the strong intuition that I had to invest myself, heart, body and soul, to embrace life in order to find the truth that I had desperately been looking for. I understood at that moment, and perhaps for the first time, that one of the main aims of ayahuasca ceremonies is to develop the honest seeker's willpower. Strangely, I realized that even if having faith in someone or something had its place in one's spiritual growth, nothing is more important and sacred than to believe in one's own abilities. The objective of this process is to allow us to find the path to the soul, the path to Spiritual Autonomy.

The Sun was again shining in my sky.

When I exited the small wooden cabin, I had the indescribable feeling that I was a new man, that I had risen from my ashes.

On the outskirts of the hut, I saw Aesha. I smiled broadly at her while mentally uttering: "I am feeling better now. Thank you for everything." She answered with a smile. In the canteen, I saw Scott. "Brother, thank you for everything. I am well now. I will tell you about it later," I told him while tapping his shoulder. He also replied with a smile. We never talked about that day, but I think he understood.

There was no ceremony the following evening, much to the relief of everyone, even to the bravest amongst us.

❄ ❄ ❄

The next morning, with my eyes barely open, all kinds of thoughts invaded my mind. Amongst them were plans for the future, judgments regarding the past events, and regrets. That morning, however, I did not analyze them. I watched them one after the other without any particular emotion. Unexpectedly, they disappeared just as they had appeared. Realizing that for years I had fruitlessly invested myself intellectually and emotionally in each of them, I smiled. This time, I forced myself not to judge my thoughts. I forced myself to live in the present moment. I was in a state of blissful peace.

At breakfast, sitting amongst my friends and without much effort, I experienced each moment with a new intensity. I was present. Through our discussions, it became obvious that I had spent a considerable amount of energy judging everything and everyone for too long, excluding myself from everything and everyone, resulting in a life of impenetrable solitude. At present, what my friends were expressing through their words, smiles, expressions, and gestures showed a whole new dimension. Somehow, they were telling me that, just like me, they had countless questions; just like me, they were feeling abandoned, they were suffering and looking for the same answers as I was; just like me, they battled with the only tools they had to become better, more loving, and more genuine beings. At present, I was a part of their life. I belonged to a whole. I did not judge my friends anymore. I did not judge myself anymore. Perhaps for the first time in my life, I was under the impression that I was genuine and authentic.

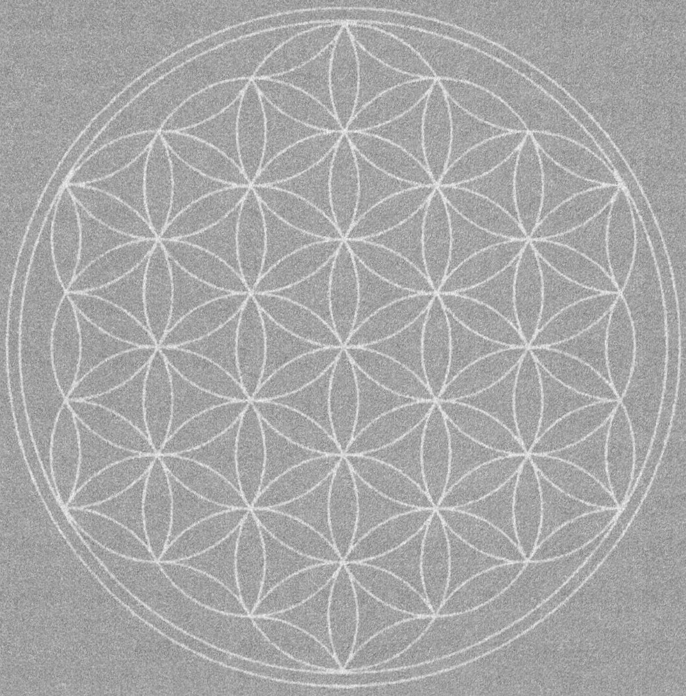

The Inner Path

The inner path is always solitary and sunny.
It requires vigilance at all times;
to see and to hear the signs that the sky and life offer;
to accept or to grab the invitations and gifts with your hands held out.
—Jacqueline Kelen

November 24, 2016

No ceremony was held for our group that evening. The Russian camera crew had organized a private ceremony for their documentary. This gave even the bravest of us great relief. I went to bed early and although it was uncomfortably hot, I fell asleep without trouble.

❄ ❄ ❄

It was still night-time when I reopened my eyes. I was sweating profusely and could hardly breathe. It seemed that I had just left a nightmare in which I must have been imprisoned in a confined space because when I woke up, I experienced an intense feeling of claustrophobia. Panic-stricken, I jumped out of my hammock then desperately tried to exit the mosquito net. After several attempts, I found the zip flap and slid it enough to free myself from the shackles of my imaginary prison. I struggled to catch my breath. My heart was beating wildly.

When I was a child and until the age of six or seven, I often had these same panic attacks. Lying on my back and just a few moments before falling asleep, I would suddenly feel like I was freefalling backwards, as if I had been sucked in by the mattress. I would need to open my eyes to drag myself out of the unpleasant sensation and resulting uncontrollable fear. Over time, I tried to control my fear to go further into the experience, but I was never able to know if there was a final destination, or an exit, because I would keep falling endlessly, it seemed. The fear would invariably make me open my eyes when it became unbearable. When I closed them again and after a few deep breaths, I would finally fall asleep.

Still on my feet in front of the mosquito net, I thought that I could return to sleep by lying in my tent, which I hastened to do. However, as soon as my eyes closed, an intense feeling of falling backwards made me reopen them abruptly. I reiterated the attempt several times while trying to control my thoughts and fear and by breathing deeply, but the result was invariably the same: sensation of freefalling like an express elevator. After the last time I tried, my heart was racing, I was choking.

I exited the hut to walk around. The air was fresh. Hernan was sitting on the steps of the hut. He had not been feeling well for two days. We thought that it was mild indigestion, but with all the pills he had taken, he should have been feeling better by now, which was visibly not the case. Hernan is normally a very jovial person. He is undoubtedly the most positive person I have ever met. Everyone loves his beautiful character.

"I am going to die, brother. This is it…" He said with a nervous smile.

"Hmm… What are you feeling, brother?"

"My whole body is in pain. I've had diarrhea for two days. I have to go to the toilet every five minutes, but nothing comes out. I constantly sweat, I shiver, and I am cold. My stomach also hurts. I have no energy. I think that I have caught malaria."

"Oh… No, it can't be that, brother. Do you want me to get the doctor?"

"I am tired of all of these doctors, with their pills… I cannot take it anymore. This damned[1] jungle is going to get me. I want to go home."

"Oh, gosh… Dammed jungle. Yes! That I understand, totally!" I told him while laughing. He started to chuckle. We exchanged a few more words before he returned to his tent.

Hernan really struggled to recover. It is only after returning home and resting for two whole months that he finally started to feel better. Today, he has returned to full health.

The fatigue was gaining ground. I had another type of mosquito net in my travel bag which I had bought in a sports shop in Rio de Janeiro. It was round, could be hanged on to the ceiling, and was barely half a meter in diameter at the top and about two meters at its base once completely unfolded. I had never unwrapped it. Because of the claustrophobia that I felt in the mosquito net around the hammock and inside the tent, I decided to try it. Hooked to one of the roof's beams, I rolled it out until it touched the floor. I

---

1. He actually said 'f*cking', and so did I—pardon our French.

slid inside, then lay down on my yoga mat. "How can I panic with claustrophobia, lying on the ground, with just a fine net and without a zip 'imprisoning' me?" It seemed very improbable, I thought.

However, as soon as I closed my eyes, the feeling of being violently sucked up by the ground beneath me came back. While breathing deeply and with my eyes open, I realized that the shamanic incantations of the private ceremony had just begun. Strangely, although I had not consumed ayahuasca that evening, the incantations had a hold on me. They exerted a hypnotic pull on my mind. Closing my eyes, I saw the geometric shapes parading with their usual pride. "Gosh... Do I still have ayahuasca in my blood? No, that's impossible," I thought while panicking even more.

As I straightened up, I had the horrible feeling of being stuck between two worlds. "Is *this* the life of a human being? Being perpetually captive in a place, a situation, or a state of consciousness? While we sleep, we are prisoners of our dreams, over which we normally have no control. When we are awake, we are stuck between our physical body and our imagination. Does death hold the same cruel fate for us?" I asked myself while remembering my experiences with death under the influence of ayahuasca. "Where *is* freedom? Does it *really* exist? Are we trapped in a prison until the end of time? This makes *no* sense!" I angrily yelled. A ruthless feeling of claustrophobia took over me. I could not breathe anymore. The air became rare, to the point where my whole body shivered uncontrollably.

Then, the same voice that I had heard in the shower cabin suddenly spoke: "Close your eyes and surrender." I was astounded. After lying down and closing my eyes again, I immediately felt that I was being sucked up backwards. "Let go this time!" I ordered myself. I then hurtled down a tunnel at full speed. It was pitch black. An ever-increasing and suffocating sensation of confinement and claustrophobia came over me. Going further and further down the endless dark tunnel, I struggled to keep my eyes closed while concentrating fully on the feeling of being sucked into the infinite hole. This time, *I had* to get to the end of whatever was there. If there was a destination, *I had* to reach it.

Suddenly and as out of nowhere, bright and vivid images appeared behind my closed eyelids. They revealed a luxuriant jungle landscape which was composed of countless shades of green, brown and yellow, emanating from an incredibly dense and thick foliage. The setting was of such surreal quality that it felt both magical and worrying. I then realized that the landscape was not static: the trees of this dense forest passed me on both sides at high speed; or rather, I was going through the landscape at full speed, as if slaloming between the trees, and that, much faster than what my eyes could grasp. The remarkable agility and incredible velocity of my movements between the powerful tree trunks indicated that I was not a human being, but a large animal galloping wildly. Through my fur, I felt the fresh waters from the large leaves on my path. The air was humid and warm, but surprisingly pleasant. My lungs were filled with it. My breathing was fast and heavy but it felt natural. From my long, precise, and quick leaps, I had a feeling of powerful and calm force. Each of my advances through the wild jungle increased my confidence.

Even though I was only a spectator and ostensibly did not have any power over the direction that this powerful animal was following, I felt that I was one with him, that I could wander to infinity, that I could express my strength without having to contain it, and that I was an integral part of Nature. I was certain that I was free, most likely for the first time in my life. I had no more doubt.

This extraordinary feeling of happiness and freedom lasted a long time. Then, the voice inside of me continued: "The only way to escape the prison in which you feel trapped in is to follow the inner path." I was stupefied. I had already heard these words before. It was precisely what a Vedanta philosophy teacher told us during one of my stays in India: "Dear friends, understand this. Why do you look for happiness outside of yourselves? There is no true happiness outside. Outside, there is nothing. Happiness is *inside* of you. Only *within* you. Understand that. The only path that leads to liberation and to the end of suffering, to genuine freedom, to sustainable happiness, is the *inner path.*"

❄ ❄ ❄

During the hours that followed this experience, I wondered about the topic of self-realization. According to Abraham Maslow, people are motivated to achieve certain needs and that some needs take precedence over others. Our most basic need is for physical survival, and this is the first thing that motivates our behavior. Once that level is fulfilled the next level up is what motivates us, and so on. However, why do we have this innate need to go beyond physical survival? Why do we have the need to grow spiritually? What is this force which, as stated by the Indian sage, Sadhguru Jaggi Vasudev, pushes us to surpass ourselves, to become more than we are, which torments and tortures us when we do not listen to it? In other words, why can't we be satisfied with simply following our survival instincts, like animals do without torturing themselves? Ravens do not think of becoming foxes, cicadas do not want to imitate ants, and tigers do not dream of trying skydiving. Only humans have these desires and ambitions. Where do these attributes, which are so unique to the human race, come from?

We all possess a physical body. However, if that was all that defined us, we would only be a pile of flesh and would exist for a much shorter amount of time than we presently do under our climatic conditions. Besides our physical body, we are endowed with vitality, thinking capacity, memory, emotions and feelings, as well as the ability to dream and imagine. If what defined us stopped there, we would not be very different to animals.

In Rosicrucian literature, as well as in other philosophies and religious and sacred texts, it is said that each animal species is guided by a distinct Group Spirit. On the one hand, this would explain the almost identical behavior that each animal observes within their species and, on the other hand, it would explain the fact that their conducts cannot be characterized as right or wrong, because they act according to their Group Spirit, directly under the Divine Light. In these same writings, it is said that all humans possess a distinct soul, a Divine Spark on their own. Animals, just like plants and minerals, also have a Divine Spark, but it is manifested on a species level, by their Group Spirit. For human beings, however, even if the source of our divine sparks is unique, it seems that we are tasked with manifesting it individually.

When we look at humans throughout history, it is clear that the

Divine Call is not heard by and expressed through each of us with the same intensity and quality. Although we all hear it or feel it to a certain extent, it is rather obvious that many of us have become masters in the art of suffocating it to give free rein to their animal passions.

Considering the suffering and difficulties that most humans go through during their brief time on Earth, we could ask ourselves if our Creator voluntarily showed injustice and cruelty towards Its[1] Creation. The reason behind this torment is probably completely different. The state in which we find ourselves as human beings, incarnated, far away from the Divine Light, and, for most of us, incapable of clearly hearing the voice of the soul, is the result of the conflict between the two worlds—our dimensions—that we belong to: the dense world of matter and the etheric world of spirits, or the physical body and the soul, or even the ego and universal love. The suffering that we experience as incarnate beings is proportional to the intensity of the battle between our lower self—which is the physical body's incessant needs, our animal instincts, and fears— and our soul which only aspires to soar to higher heights, where unconditional love is all-pervasive.

In terms of evolution, benevolent spirits, angels, archangels, and other spiritual kingdoms are located above that of the humans, which is above that of animals. In this configuration, that is half-animal and half-angel, we occupy a particularly unique position by standing between two worlds, where we have the relative liberty to direct our thoughts, ambitions, aspirations, and actions towards one of these two kingdoms. It is at this precarious position that

---

1. Or His, or Her Creation

the soul's battle takes place. It is at this decisive crossroads that the soul either suffocates in the flesh or elevates the incarnated to the heavens. Each thought, each choice, each action, either brings us closer to the voice of the soul or takes us away from it.

In religious and philosophical literature, it is often mentioned that humans possess freewill. What is this mysterious concept? Saint Augustine stated that freewill consists of the ability that humans possess to decide freely for themselves, to act and think, contrary to determinism or fatalism. However, although it is an interesting definition, there is clear evidence that we have no choice on a large number of aspects that govern our lives. Do we have a choice on our place and time of birth, on our parents and relatives, time of death, or on other vast number of parameters that determine our existence here on Earth for the most part? Evidently not. Therefore, what is this concept of freewill? Is it to decide our profession, our life partner, to be materially rich or poor, to become famous or remain anonymous? It seems unlikely because all of these choices are connected to the era in which we live as well as our geographical location. So again, what is this freewill about?

Humans were bestowed with freewill to choose the direction in which they guide their thoughts, ambitions, aspirations, and actions throughout their life as incarnate souls. Will they use this faculty to satisfy their lower nature or will they do so with the aim of elevating themselves to the heavens, to unconditional love? Will they allow themselves to be governed by their animal passions or will they listen to the voice of their soul? This *is* freewill.

Where we are, between two worlds, half-animal and half-angel, the choice is ours.

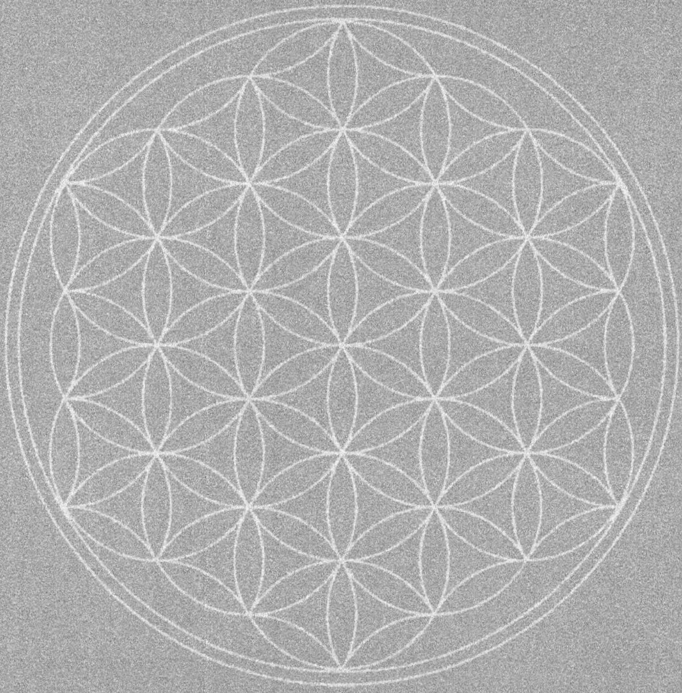

The Curious Role of the Ego

Be the master of your heart, not the slave of your ego.
—Paulo Coelho

November 26, 2016

My heart was heavy as I was sitting on the small wooden chair in the center of the maloca, with my voice recorder in my hand. I felt battered and bruised. Before taking part in this long journey in the Amazon forest, I had pictured that the ceremonies were going to take me to faraway lands where I would converse with my spiritual guides or celestial angels in order to finally find an explanation about Life, the reason why there is so much suffering on Earth, and the causes of so much apparent injustice in my life. I was evidently million miles away from imagining that what I was going to find here, in the merciless jungle, would be vastly different.

During these ceremonies, ayahuasca dragged me by force to the depths of my soul that had been unknown to me up to that point. Had I consciously avoided these dangerous abysses before? If that was the case, had I done it for fear of what I could have found? I had no idea, but the result was there, and I was suffering terribly from it.

For many years and during my countless musings, I had sensed that something inside of me prevented me from being the person that I longed to be. I felt as if I was a prisoner in an impenetrable shell that kept me away from the genuine and loving person I aspired to be, that kept me away from genuine happiness. I subconsciously knew that if I succeeded in breaking this seemingly indestructible shell, I could become that person. It would finally be possible for me to see the light of my soul, which is absolutely fundamental in the fulfillment of all incarnate beings. I was now fully aware that this part of me, which I had accused of being my enemy, was my ego. But what was this *ego*? Also, how could it have become so important, so predominant in my life, without me noticing?

According to the famous Swiss psychiatrist and therapist, Carl Jung, the ego is the seat of human consciousness. It is from there that humans experience the incarnate existence during which they create their own identity. At birth, a child does not have predefined behavior. It develops depending on the surroundings and the events that occur throughout life. It is the behavior resulting from human experience that creates and gives substance to the ego. The ego is a purely mental and individual creation.

Jung states that the ego develops in two stages. During childhood, it constitutes a mechanism that naturally establishes itself to protect the child from the hostile environment during the growth and learning period. It also enables interaction with the surrounding world, allowing the child to survive and operate in society. In adulthood, the ego serves additional functions, such as satisfying various physiological needs, safety and social insertion, as well as the function of logical reasoning. These mechanisms are clearly essential for humans to function properly and to integrate their environment.

However, once sheltered from the dangers of the environment and after taking a role in the society to which they belong, humans should naturally feel the need to seek the true meaning of life. Once their personality is well integrated, they should feel their soul calling, giving them the strength that is required to reach self-realization. It is only at this moment that their spiritual development can begin. Jung observed that the first part of our life is dedicated to shape the ego, and the second part to rid of it. The distinguished psychiatrist noted that this behavior is completely normal for a human in a healthy mental condition.

A question naturally arises: why does such a mechanism exist in humans if not to indicate that the time for spiritual growth has arrived? Is this process not the outward manifestation of a distressed soul? Yet, although the answer is almost self-evident, one could ask whether today the distress signal is powerful enough to quiet down the ego. Lost and too invested in our chaotic societies, can we still hear the faint voice? It is undeniable that the economy that governs our modern societies has contributed enormously to the indulgence and gratification of the ego[1]. The infernal economic machinery has insidiously reduced us to a product of society. The result is that today, instead of serving us, the ego enslaves us. We have become its prey and toy to such an extent that many of us can only be liberated from its powerful grip at the time of physical death.

---

1. On this subject, watch the BBC documentary series by Adam Curtis, *The Century of the Self*, 2002

Our seemingly important role in society, the relative power that we possess, the fame and recognition that we receive, and the attachment to our social image and position have taken such a prominent position that we are no longer aware of who we truly are. We have forgotten that, above all, we are a Soul, a Divine Spark, Consciousness. The ego's shell has become so thick, so opaque, and so rigid for most of us that the Divine Light is unable to shine through. This growing phenomenon means that instead of being a powerful tool and ally in our development here on Earth, the ego is a thick armor that keeps us away from spirituality, from a rich, loving and happy life; from Universal Love. Sadly, the ego has become the prison of the soul.

❊ ❊ ❊

Sitting on the small wooden chair in the center of the maloca, with my voice recorder in my hand, I realized the magnitude and negative proportion that my ego had taken in my life. I became aware of the indestructible shell that had taken me great effort to build and countless years to mold. This impenetrable shell had kept me prisoner in a world that was impervious to genuine happiness. It had kept me away from the person I wanted to be, far from the person I really was. I also realized, with bitterness and pain, that the unbearable solitude that had accompanied me for all these years was not due to factors outside of my will or to a cosmic conspiracy, as I had believed, but to the limited understanding that I had of spirituality and self-realization. The prison that I felt trapped in was of my own design. I became aware that I had always been part of a whole that was infinitely vaster and more charitable than my insignificant self and ruthless ego.

Sitting on the small wooden chair in the center of the maloca, with my voice recorder in my hand and tears rolling down my cheeks, I realized that ayahuasca had created a gaping hole in my ego.

As I was becoming increasingly aware of that, a slightly unpleasant tingling went through my left fingertips. It intensified slowly, then spread to my entire hand, my arm, chest, and up to my heart. The feeling was akin to electricity flowing through the entire left side of my body. I then had strong palpitations, followed by pins and needles up to the tip of my left toes. I was under the impression that I was recharged with energy. The persistent pain that I had felt in the left side of my chest for several days faded, then disappeared. I then experienced a feeling of peace and infinite presence.

Although there was one more ayahuasca ceremony that I could participate in, I knew that my journey in the Amazon had just ended. Before the last few ceremonies, I was often undecided as to whether or not I should drink ayahuasca. I did eventually consume it for fear of having regrets the next day, thinking that I was going to miss an opportunity to learn more. This time, sitting on the small chair in the center of the maloca, I had no more hesitation. Deep down, I knew that I had received the teaching that I had come here for.

Taken over by an irresistible urge to sleep, I lay on the ground just where I was, two feet away from the small worn-out chair. The feeling of the soft and fine sand on my skin transported me outside of the hot and humid jungle. As I let out a very long sigh, my heavy eyelids closed.

I was truly in peace, most likely for the first time in my long life.

PRACTICAL CEREMONY AND INTEGRATION GUIDE WITH AYAHUASCA

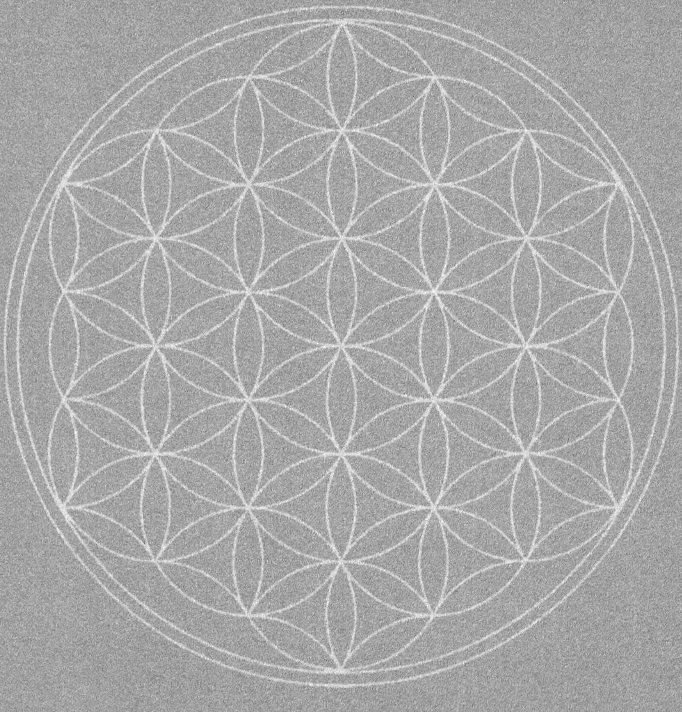

The Dangers of Ayahuasca

July 2017 — eight months after my stay in the Amazon

Closing these chapters without adding a few words about the dangers that you can expose yourself to during ayahuasca ceremonies would be, in my opinion, a serious omission. Although ayahuasca has undeniable attributes that can improve or recover physical and mental health, and help spiritual development, I have to mention some of the dangers that this age-old practice can present if you do not prepare yourself or take any precautions. Shamans have always been aware of this. That is why they prepare and train the inhabitants of the village or villages that they are in charge of from a very early age. Unfortunately, it is rarely the case for busy Western people who are desperately seeking for spiritual growth or escape.

The problem of dependency

Even if it is just for a few hours or a few moments, escaping reality, being overtaken by a powerful benevolent force, feeling different, or being transported into a foreign dimension is a concept that entices many people, especially nowadays. Ayahuasca offers these possibilities and many more. There is a myriad of accounts regarding internal transformations and miraculous recoveries in specialized literature, and they are starting to appear on the Internet.

As I have already mentioned in the introduction, ayahuasca, like most psychedelic substances, is neither poisonous nor addictive. However, it must be noted that a substance or element that is foreign to our organism does not necessarily have to be addictive for us to be dependent on it, if only on an emotional level. The best examples of this are addictions to matters such as money, success, power, physical or emotional attachment to a person, food, habits, and many other domains.

Unfortunately, it is not uncommon to see that ayahuasca presents a significant risk of emotional attachment. Although shamanism and ayahuasca do not come from any religion or sect, it is frequently noted that a growing number of participants in ayahuasca ceremonies tend to behave like religious devotees or even fanatics in the most extreme cases. That is unfortunately the case for many Western people who are desperately looking for an escape from their life or for spiritual growth. It is also common to meet participants who only swear by the sacred plant, so much so that they are unable to conceive a future without it. Every emotion, thought, decision, and step has to be approved by the spirit of the divine plant. The emotional dependency that certain people manifest during ayahuasca ceremonies is sometimes alarming.

Any type of strong attachment represents an obstacle to spiritual development, and it is only possible to free yourself from it if you express a willingness to do so. However, if we observe most humans, we can see that one of the qualities that often fails us *is* willpower. Consequently, it is much easier to take the path of laziness, of following the animal passions, or of emotional or material attachment than to listen to the whispers of the soul. What do people who achieve greatness in the fields of spirituality or those who do so in the business world have in common? *Willpower.* This quality is so crucial to our spiritual growth that it seems our passage on Earth is one of the main reasons for it. The growing problem of emotional addiction to ayahuasca cannot be addressed effectively and durably without exercising willpower.

Until quite recently, traditional Chinese, Indian, and Tibetan medicine systems all agreed on one thing: the will of the patient is an essential part of the healing process. Besides prescribing a natural, plant-based treatment, the practitioner's task also entails stimulating the patient's motivation to regain optimal health. This takes place through discussions, practical life or spiritual counseling, or recommending practices such Tai Chi, Qi Gong, or Zhan Zhuang in China, Yoga in India, Meditation in Tibet, or many other disciplines. By doing so, and in a subtle manner, the doctor's words and advice strengthen the patient's will. A few centuries ago, Western doctors also knew the importance of this part of the recovery process. Today, this notion has unfortunately disappeared from our doctors' vocabulary. If we, as a human race, do not take notice and act upon this growing phenomenon, ayahuasca will soon be added to the existing long list of drugs or dependencies that afflict our lives.

Shamanism with ayahuasca should be used with the aim of opening the mind. In other words, it should initially be used to break the thick intellectual shell and fears—the ego—that keeps us away from the soul's callings. Once the ego is more or less out of the way, ayahuasca should only be consumed to purify or refine certain aspects of the personality or aid the process of internal transformation. Ayahuasca should *never* be used as the *sole* vehicle of knowledge and exploration or, obviously, as a recreational psychedelic journey. In that sense, ayahuasca can be compared to a teacher: the most brilliant of instructors can teach their students how to make the best use of the tools that they have at their disposal, but they will never be able to use these tools for the students when the time comes. Similarly, if they are properly held, ayahuasca ceremonies can facilitate the spiritual development of those who have the strong desire to grow, but they will *never* be able to go on the journey of spiritual realization for them.

One day, a good shaman friend told me that ayahuasca yields the best results for people who have their feet firmly rooted on the ground. He added, "Interestingly, with ayahuasca, it is those who have their feet firmly rooted on the ground that reach the highest peaks."

The existential crisis

One of ayahuasca's characteristic effects is to offer a new perspective of the world, a new reality. During the few hours (in general, four to six) that follow the absorption of the fearsome brew, the understanding that we have of ordinary reality and the markers that we were accustomed to are shaken, or even turned upside down. Because of this, at the end of a ceremony, it is not uncommon for a considerable number of participants to hastily decide to radically transform their lives. This behavior very often leads to spectacular, even dramatic decisions: divorce, change of job, impulsive sales or donations of personal possessions, exodus in the forest or a remote place on top of a mountain, tattoos from head to toe, sex change, unbridled participation in dangerous activities, etc. That may be the solution for some people, but for many, the result is often tragic.

In adulthood, most of us operate with ease in society, going about our mundane and daily routines. However, it must be noted that these activities or rituals, though seemingly basic, require years and years of practice. The same can be said for ayahuasca; under its influence, when we operate for the first time or the first times in the meanders of the new reality that is presented to us, we are just like newborns, lost in a world that infinitely surpasses us. Consequently, this is mainly where one of the biggest dangers of ayahuasca lies.

It is very likely that the main intention of these shamanic practices is to open the door to the spirit world, as Huxley stated. That is why you often hear participants say that the information they received was timely, perhaps even crucial, for their spiritual development. However, given that the process is relatively brutal and works in a way that does not always make sense to a novice, at the end of an ayahuasca ceremony, you should give yourself time to *think carefully before acting*. In the next chapter, we will discuss an exercise that aims to help the participant improve the decision process after an ayahuasca ceremony.

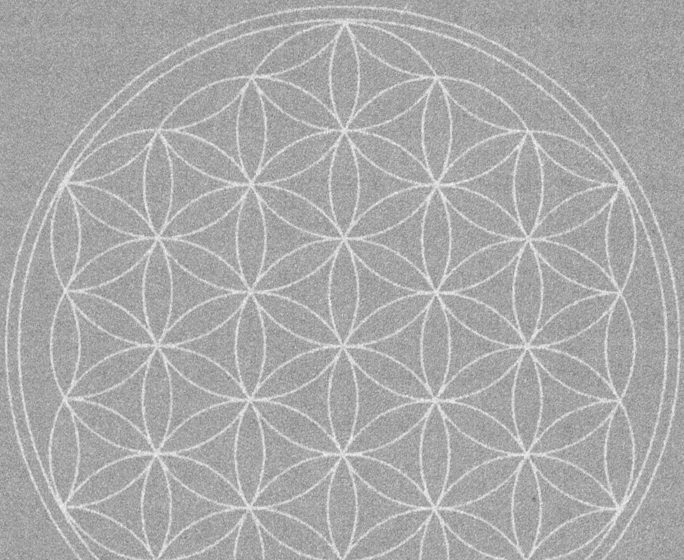

The Ayahuasca Integration Phase

July 2017, Bali, Indonesia

During the months following my departure from the jungle, I tried to write my experiences down on paper. The emotions generated from this exercise were so intense and painful, however, that I had to stop several times. My initial intention was not to write a book, but rather to prevent myself from forgetting the important points that ayahuasca ceremonies and the people whom I met taught me, and also to give a meaning to this adventure that could satisfy my left brain—my intellect.

Today, besides these two aspects, I know that I needed to undertake this task. In a way, it was my personal way to review my life, to heal, and to grow. A shaman, who has since become a good friend, told me during an interview, "The true work with ayahuasca begins *after* the ceremony." I now know that these words were full of wisdom. In shamanic circles, this phase, during which the participant feels the benefits of the ceremony or ceremonies that they have just taken part in, is called 'Integration'. However, because this phase is generally long, laborious, and painful, it is very often ignored, or hastily shortened at best, which is obviously a mistake and does have negative consequences. The ayahuasca integration phase is, to a large extent, even more important than the ceremony for any honest spiritual seeker.

Although there is no ready-made formula to integrate the experiences that you have lived and the information that you have received during ayahuasca ceremonies, following is an exercise that I developed the habit of doing after each ceremony[1]. It goes without saying that this practice helped me greatly interpret and open a path for myself in the complex world of shamanism and ayahuasca. Although I am by no means an expert in this field, I sincerely hope that it will help you.

Practice that facilitates the integration phase after an ayahuasca ceremony

First of all, it is important that the exercise detailed here be performed alone, in a calm place, sheltered from distractions and indiscreet looks. Also, until you have fully carried this exercise out, do not mention it to anyone, not even your loved ones. I say this for several reasons:

1. Firstly, not to waste your 'energy' (or 'Qi', as it is called in Chinese philosophy);

2. Secondly, let your intuition guide you—and not your family, friends, surroundings, ego or intellect;

3. And finally, to increase your spiritual autonomy.

1. Taking notes

During my stay in the Amazon, I noticed that some of the moments that I had lived or certain information that I had received during an ayahuasca ceremony did not necessarily have an obvious meaning. It only appeared clearly to me after a few days, weeks, or

---

1. I developed this practice in 2017, between the 2016 Huni Kuin Brazil festival and another long ayahuasca retreat I did in Peru, Iquitos.

even longer in some cases. Consequently, after each ceremony, I developed the habit of writing down my sensations, the contents of my visions, the advice that I received, the important points during conversations with friends, as well as my personal thoughts, reaction and emotions. Looking back, I realize that a lot of the events that take place during a ceremony have a meaning, as insignificant as it may seem at first.

As a result, take the time to write all of the events, sensations, and visions that manifested themselves under the influence of ayahuasca immediately after a ceremony and in as much detail as possible. Note your thoughts during the day following the ceremony as well. Finally, take note of the conversations and words exchanged with the other participants, the organizers, and the shamans during and after the ceremony.

Use a voice recorder, if needed, not to lose track of your ideas while transcribing them—I mostly use this method because it allows me to listen to my own voice and emotions at the time. Make sure that you transcribe the points that seem the most important to you *very quickly after the ceremony*.

2. Period of reflection

As we have already addressed in the previous chapter, *do not make any rash decisions immediately after a ceremony*. This advice is also valid after taking notes with the help of the instructions above. At this stage, it is very important to give yourself a period of reflection. This can be half a day, a day, a week, or even longer. In my experience, the longer the better.

Listen to yourself. Follow your intuition.

3. Envisaged decisions or changes

During this time, while remembering the information gathered during the past ceremony, compile a list with the changes that you would like to make in your life as well as the blockages that seemingly prevent you from being happy or from achieving the goal that you have set for yourself. Do this on paper.

I voluntarily use the adverb 'seemingly' here because you could be surprised to see that what you thought to be primordial can find itself at the bottom of the list at the end of this exercise. If it is not the first time that you are doing this exercise, note that it is not necessary to list the same points that have a connection with those from your notes of the past ceremonies. If you feel that you have to, however, let it be so.

This is important: before starting, *do not read* the notes that you wrote about the past ceremony or ceremonies.

In order to be as concrete as possible regarding this first list, which we will call it List of Decisions, here is an example:

L1. Example of a List of Decisions

> 1 –> Change jobs
>
> 2 –> Sell the house
>
> 3 –> Tell Pablo that I did not appreciate his remark
>
> 4 –> Call Claudine to apologize
>
> 5 –> Buy a new car
>
> 6 –> Sign up to the library
>
> 7 –> Get a tattoo of a dragon on the left shoulder

4. Intuitive development

Next, proceed as follows: take as many blank sheets of paper as there are points on your List of Decisions. With the example above, we have gathered seven sheets of paper. Each of them will be what we will call an Intuitive Development.

At the top of each of these sheets, write one of the points of your List of Decisions. With our example, we have written 'Change jobs' on the first sheet of Intuitive Development, 'Sell the house' on the second sheet, and so on until the seventh sheet, which contains 'Get a tattoo of a dragon on the left shoulder'.

Then, take one of these Intuitive Development sheets and ask yourself why what you have written down on it is important. *Do not analyze your answer*, this is about letting your *intuition* guide you, and not your ego or intellect. Once you have obtained the answer, write it just below.

Proceed in the same manner and ask yourself about the relevance and importance of this new intuitive answer. Keep doing this until you are satisfied and become aware of something interesting or that resonates in you.

Write as many points as you think are necessary. There is no limit as to maximum length.

For example, regarding the second point of our List of Decisions, titled 'Sell the house', you could proceed in the following manner:

L2. Example of an Intuitive Development sheet (obtained intuitively from the second point of the List of Decisions)

2 –> <u>Sell the house</u>

- Why do you want to sell the house?

  -> I want to leave this place

- Why do you want to leave here?

  -> I feel like a prisoner inside of this house

- Why do feel like a prisoner inside of this house?

  -> I cannot come out of my shell

- Why can't you come out of your shell?

  -> I feel lonely, I don't have any friends

- Why don't you have any friends?

  -> I don't get out enough

- Why do you not get out enough, what are you afraid of?

  -> I don't know, I feel like I am incapable of loving and being loved

5. Answers obtained intuitively

At this point, you should have as many Intuitive Development sheets as there are points on your List of Decisions.

Take another blank sheet of paper, which we will call List of Intuitive Answers, and write the last point of each sheet of Intuitive Development on it.

Here is an example obtained from our seven sheets of Intuitive Development:

L3. Example of a List of Intuitive Answers

- I like people, I want to be a psychologist

- I don't know, I feel like I am incapable of loving and being loved [note: obtained above, from 2 –> <u>Sell the house</u>]

- My parents have never understood me

- I feel like I am incapable of loving and being loved

- I feel like a prisoner, I feel like I am incapable of loving and being loved

- I feel like a prisoner, I feel like I am incapable of loving and being loved

- I feel imprisoned

6. Unique intuitive answers

Once you have made your List of Intuitive Answers, reread it and remove the duplicates, if any.

Here is an example of List of Unique Intuitive Answers obtained from our List of Intuitive Answers:

L4. Example of List of Unique Intuitive Answers

- I like people, I want to be a psychologist

- ~~I don't know,~~ I feel like I am incapable of loving and being loved

- My parents have never understood me

- ~~I feel like I am incapable of loving and being loved~~

- I feel like a prisoner, ~~I feel like I am incapable of loving and being loved~~

- ~~I feel like a prisoner, I feel like I am incapable of loving and being loved~~

• I feel imprisoned

7. Reflection on the intuitive answers obtained

While browsing the answers obtained this way, try to reach a conclusion *intuitively*, which means without soliciting reason and analysis.

If you are unable to do so the first time, do not be discouraged, because this is an exercise that requires patience and perseverance. When you reach an interesting conclusion, write it on this final list and think about it deeply for a little while every day, but remember: try to avoid reason and analysis.

You can use the tables at the end of the book to complete this exercise.

8. Dig deeper

If you have not obtained any pertinent information at the end of this process, repeat the whole exercise with your final list, the List of Unique Intuitive Answers—L4—as the starting point. In other words, make this list a new List of Decisions—L1. Then, proceed as we did previously, from L2 to L4, to make a set of sheets of Intuitive Development, then a List of Intuitive Answers, and finally, a List of Unique Intuitive Answers.

Repeat this process until you reach a set of answers which you do not think can be narrowed down further.

Ideally, you want to obtain one unique answer at the end, but this does not seem absolutely necessary to reap the benefits of this practice.

9. Practice makes perfect

Repeat this exercise at least three times over the following weeks. The sessions should ideally be spaced a week apart from each other. However, if the ceremonies in which you participate are close together, do this exercise depending on the time that you have. When I was in the Amazon forest[1], I did not have the luxury of thinking and meditating for a week after each ceremony. I only had forty-eight hours to do this exercise. It still proved to be very effective.

10. Emotions, reason, and intuition

Generally speaking, when we make a decision, our emotions, reason, and intuition should be used equally in order to reach an ideal or even satisfactory result. Ideally, we should be guided by intuition, by the voice of the soul, but most of us are evidently far from that. Today, it must be noted that emotions take center stage, followed by the intellect far behind, then intuition, located even further away, subdued, tamed, and pushed back in a dark place. The true aim of the above exercise is to free the decision-making process as much as possible from two important constraints: intense emotions and the rational and often too analytical intellect.

11. Ayahuasca and spirituality

To close this chapter and the one preceding it, note that the shamanic practice with ayahuasca initially operates through in-depth work on our physical body and its physiological components, our emotions, and our mind. This work is carried out thanks to detoxification, purification, regeneration, and harmonization techniques and exercises. During this process, people often report renewed

---

1. In 2017, in Peru, Iquitos.

vital forces, freedom from emotional knots, awakening of spiritual abilities, and the discovery of the hidden meaning of our inner nature. Once freed from these blockages and connected once more to the universe that surrounds us, we can reconnect ourselves to our higher self, to our soul.

During your research and shamanic practices with ayahuasca, keep in mind that the ultimate goal of this age-old practice is to help us achieve spiritual autonomy.

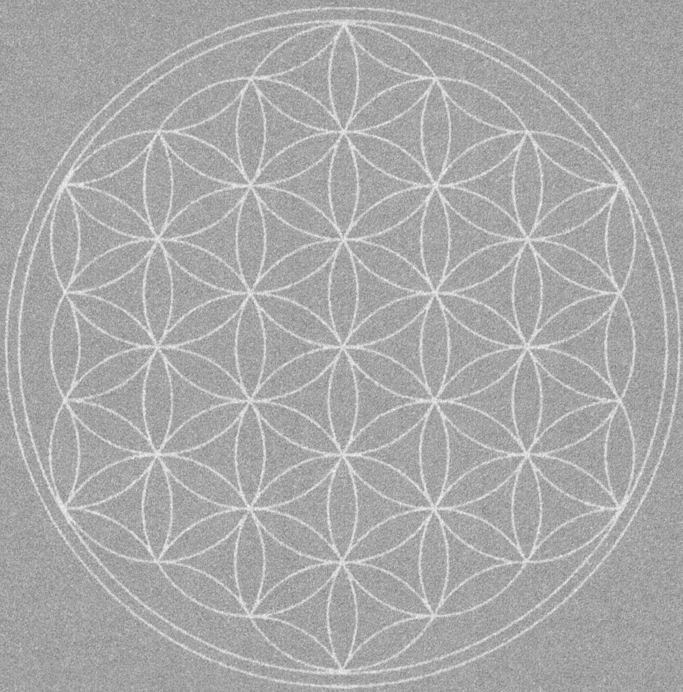

A Practical Guide to
Ayahuasca Ceremonies

1. Ayahuasca in the eyes of the law

On February 21, 1971, a conference in Vienna led to the signing of an agreement that included almost all mind-altering substances. This agreement, which contains restrictions regarding importation and exportation as well as other rules that aim to limit the consumption of drugs to scientific or medical purposes, became effective from August 16, 1976. Today (2018), 175 nations have signed this agreement.

Although the effectiveness of ayahuasca in the healing process of certain physical and mental diseases has been proven for several years by a growing number of serious scientific studies carried out by universities in the United States, South America (notably in Brazil, Peru, and Colombia), Europe and other countries, its consumption and usage are illegal in almost every country. In France, for instance, most of the plants that are used to prepare ayahuasca have been illegal since 2005.

Know that laws change over time, however. Therefore, before leaving, inquire about the destination where you plan to participate in ayahuasca ceremonies and its applicable laws. In most countries, ayahuasca is considered to be a narcotic drug and is therefore illegal. The penalties can be very severe and deadly in some cases (i.e.

Malaysia, Singapore, China and many others).

2. Your health condition

Before taking the plunge into an ayahuasca ceremony, consult your doctor and make sure that you are in excellent health condition.

Ayahuasca is very strongly discouraged (or forbidden most of the time by the organizers and shamans of serious centers) in the following cases:

- Psychological conditions, such as schizophrenia, bipolarity, and psychosis;

- Heart diseases;

- Epilepsy;

- Liver and kidney problems;

- Diabetes;

- During pregnancy.

As a rule, do not take any medication or synthetic drugs for at least a month before consuming ayahuasca. If you have a particular health problem, it is **important to personally** contact a competent authority about how your organism could react to ayahuasca, then inform the center that you are going to. Remember that a large number of diseases that affect us and medication that we use today do not exist in the Amazon. Therefore, the shamans will most probably not be able to advise you correctly, hence do some serious research before leaving. Also know that if ayahuasca is discouraged or forbidden for you to consume, there are other medicinal plants or shamanic techniques that can be used for a specific cure or to help you grow spiritually.

3. Before the departure

3.1. Carry out in-depth research

The phenomenon of 'ayahuasca tourism', which is now growing aggressively, has negative repercussions on this age-old practice. Therefore, research in depth the organizations in the country or city that you have selected. The fact that 'ayahuasca healing center' appears at the top of a Google search and that it is located in an attractive location is in no way a guarantee of quality, nor does it necessarily mean that it will suit you. Some of these centers organize ceremonies with more than twenty people in an attempt to maximize profit, at the expense of quality. Generally speaking, the lower the number of participants allowed, the more attention the shaman and the organizers will give to you and the more intimacy and deep bonds between the participants will be created.

Read the comments left by the participants of past ceremonies on the forums provided for this purpose on the Internet. In my opinion, the safest option is to join a known group that has been around for several years—not to say decades. You have nothing to prove to anyone or to yourself. If you have personal pride, a strong ego, or something to prove to your loved ones, be careful this time, **do not fear being too cautious**. This is about your own mental and physical health.

3.2. Choose your shaman

Note that it is not because a shaman suits someone that they will necessarily suit you. Shamans generally specialize in a type of physical or mental illness, or deal with heartbreak, existential problems, the cries of the soul, breaking spells, as well as many other fields. Although a shaman has been able to give one of your close friends the experience that they were looking for, it is possible that the shaman is unable to do the same for you. Finally, not all shamans have the same techniques or work with same plant families.

Also, keep in mind that the shamans are humans first and foremost. They are not perfect and do not all perform miracles. If you have the time, patience, and opportunity, partake in ceremonies with some highly recommended shamans. For some, you will find information about them by consulting the website of the center where they work. Try to get an interview with your shaman or with the organizers before your first ceremony.

3.3. You are going alone, be even more careful

If you decide to travel alone, be especially cautious. When you reach your destination, do not hesitate to ask the foreign community and the locals for advice. While walking down the streets looking for a shaman, if you hear someone shout, 'Ayahuasca!', it is very likely for profit. Many of these 'ayahuasca sellers' will take you to people who are not real shamans. Having twenty or forty years' experience with ayahuasca does not make someone a shaman. If you feel that something is not right, run. **Follow your intuition**.

3.4. Inform the center of your health condition

Whether you are going alone or in a group, it is **crucial** to inform the organizers or the shamans of the chosen center about the medication that you are taking or took in the past. Do not be shy.

Indeed, ayahuasca **should not** be consumed if you take certain natural or artificial substances, treatments, or medication, especially **antidepressants**. These can lead to serotonin syndrome, which is an adverse and potentially fatal effect which is linked to the disturbance of the chemical balance and the central nervous system due to an excess of serotonin in the brain. A substantial amount of bad press surrounding ayahuasca and deaths have been reported, but the fact that the deceased was taking antidepressants before the ceremony is rarely mentioned.

It has also been reported that people who take vitamin supplements did not feel the effects of ayahuasca.

3.5. List of items to take with you

If you go to the Amazon, here is a list of the items to take with you.

- A hammock

- A mosquito net (to put around your hammock)

- A tent (to sleep in it or store your belongings)

- An air mattress with its pillow (self-inflating or not)

- A hiking backpack that can hold 70 to 120 liters (avoid suitcases with wheels)

- A hat or cap (if you can, pick a model with a mosquito net)

- Rubber mid-calf boots (to walk in the forest)

- Long and short trousers

- Long-sleeve and short-sleeve shirts

- A raincoat or waterproof coat (preferably with a hood)

- A microfiber hand towel

- Swimming trunks or shorts

- An umbrella

- A durable plastic glass or cup

- A flask (I highly recommend the LifeStraw brand in particular, available on Amazon, or an equivalent flask)

- Natural insecticide, like lemongrass, neem oil, tea tree, or witch-hazel (although not very effective against sand fleas)

- Soothing cream for itches caused by insect bites

- A paper dictionary and conversation guide in the target language (even if you have an equivalent mobile application on your mobile phone)

- A set of travel cutlery

- A watch

- A small compass

- A small, foldable survival knife

- Toilet paper

- A lighter

- A headlamp with a set of batteries or a spare battery

- A few books or an e-reader, such as a Kindle/iPad (to pass the time because the days can be very long in the jungle)

- A notepad and some pens (to write your experience)

- A voice recorder

- A first-aid kit

- If you can, get a small waterproof carry case to put your important papers, phone, and small electronic accessories in (I recommend the XSories - Black Box IP 67 model or an equivalent model on Amazon)

- A universal plug adaptor

- A 10,000 mAh solar charger to charge your phone or e-reader if there is no power available (the Innoo Tech and Hiluckey brands offer perfectly suitable models)

- A flashlight

- A yoga mat (or another type of mat) for the ceremonies

3.6. Gifts for the shamans, elders, villagers, and children

In indigenous tradition, when you arrive in the village where you are going to participate in ayahuasca ceremonies, you are going to meet the shaman or shamans as well as the elders. Keep in mind that for these people, the ceremonies are spiritually very important and sacred. It is a tradition to offer a gift of gratitude and to show your respect and appreciation for the work that they do. Here are a few examples of appropriate gifts:

To the spiritual guides or the shamans of the village, offer something that concerns spirituality, shamanism, or any mystical tradition. This can be totems, pictures of saints, incenses, smoke pipes, ceremonial clothes, shamanic care items, crystals, hunting knives or Swiss Army knives, flashlights, or anything that seems appropriate to you.

For elderly women, bring a nice towel, a long skirt, a T-shirt, a dress, or any type of clothing that you like.

Offer multicolored pearls, Indian-style shawls, make-up, or anything that seems appropriate to you to the women and young women of the village.

Although children love sweets, avoid bringing any, for two reasons. Firstly, the children of the Amazon villages are not used to consuming as much sugar as we are. While they have more vitality and are in better health than our children in many aspects, they are more sensitive to chemicals. This does not mean that they never consume sweets, but they eat very little compared to our children. Furthermore, with Amazonians' teeth generally being healthy until a very old age, there are not many dentists in the Amazon. The second reason is that given that the inhabitants of the villages generally do not have a concept of biodegradability, you risk finding sweet and chocolate wrappers spread across the village and its surroundings. Bring toys, coloring books, notepads so they can draw (you could bring a few drawings back with you as a souvenir), coloring pencils, puzzles or other patience games, pens, footballs or tennis balls, or any other object that allows you to interact with these adorable children.

Also, once you have offered your gifts to the elders and shamans, do not hand out the rest of them randomly during the first few days. Offer them as the ceremonies go by, when your heart suggests it. These offerings can also be used to acquire certain shamanic objects that you like. Shamans generally like this practice, as it allows them to obtain objects that they would struggle to acquire in the forest.

3.7. Diet to follow before the ceremony

Some people will tell you that the 'dieta'—or diet—to follow before ayahuasca ceremonies is not *really* important. This is a mistake. For one, this practice reduces the number of trips to the toilet during the inevitable purge triggered by ayahuasca, and it will also ensure better mental control during visions or other states of consciousness. Certain centers go as far as starving their guests. Although their reasons are justified within certain shamanic practices, they can prove to be harmful to a novice who is too preoccupied with their empty stomach.

Here is the diet that is generally recommended by many shamanic centers:

One month before the ceremony

A month before the ceremony, stop consuming red meat (especially pork), coffee, alcohol, and it goes without saying, **all drugs**, whatever they may be.

Two weeks before the ceremony

In addition to the instructions above, avoid:

- All sexual activities, including masturbation
- Spicy food
- Ice cream and ice-cold drinks

One week before the ceremony

In addition to the instructions above, avoid:

- Refined sugars

- Pre-cooked meals, canned food, and all fast food

- Salt and pepper

- Sweets and chocolate

- Oil (if you have to use some, use olive oil or coconut oil sparingly)

- Animal fats (lard, etc.)

- Soft drinks (including fizzy drinks, energy drinks, and non-alcohol beer)

- Dairy products

- Fermented foods

- Caffeine and other stimulants

4. Before the ceremony

4.1. Dress code, ornaments, and shamanic objects

Dress lightly, in long sleeves and trousers, but bring a sweater or jacket because the temperatures drop considerably during the night in the Amazon. Wearing black during ceremonies is not recommended.

Avoid presenting yourself to the shaman while wearing tracksuits, sports clothes, or shorts. Keep in mind that an ayahuasca ceremony is a sacred and highly spiritual moment for the shamans, the villagers, as well as most participants.

Many participants wear a feather hat, adorn themselves with jewelry, bracelets, and necklaces, don a ceremonial tunic or paint their face or entire body with multicolored shamanic patterns. Some bring bones, perfume, incense, flowers, and shamanic totems. Although each of these items has its own place in the shaman's or seasoned practitioner's panoply, their description and use are far out of the context of this book. Before the ceremony, ask the organizers about what you should bring with you and what you should wear.

4.2. The intention

An hour or two before the ceremony, isolate yourself in a calm spot. Focus on yourself. Do not waste energy and precious time chatting with friends. If you hesitate about how to behave before or during the ceremony, ask the organizers or the shamans. If no one is available, read a spiritual book, listen to soft music, meditate, and relax.

When you walk towards the shamanic circle, behave as if you were going to meet a great spiritual guide, which means humbly, filled with love and respect, silently, and with head held high. Do not forget that the aim of these practices is to **build your spiritual autonomy**, and not to make you a religious fanatic or a slave.

When you hold the glass of ayahuasca in your hands and before drinking its contents, take a few moments to concentrate on your intention, on what you want to solve, experience, or explore during the upcoming ceremony. Take your time but be as brief and concise as possible. Be realistic and tell yourself that what you are going to experience will possibly be completely different to what you have in mind. Be open. A shaman once told me: "The best thing is to say: 'Show me or make me experience what I need, here and now,' that way, you leave the doors open and never be disappointed." I think it is a very wise advice. If you do not have any particular requests, think positively while holding your glass in your hand.

4.3. The first twenty minutes

Sit down after drinking the contents of the glass held to you by the shaman. You will usually feel ayahuasca's first effects after about twenty minutes. Stay seated during this period. Do not look around. Remain present. Close your eyes and focus on yourself, meditate and stay calm. Avoid making noise and disturbing other participants. Even if ayahuasca ceremonies are not of paramount importance to you, they are for some people who have come to cure a disease that has been diagnosed as terminal by science or conventional medicine. One of these people may be sitting right next to you.

5. During the ceremony

5.1. Points to note

Here, I am going to repeat the very precious advice that has been given to me by my benevolent friends during ayahuasca ceremonies.

- Avoid lying down

- Remain seated with your back straight

- Keep your eyes open

- Concentrate on your breathing

- If you are a novice, do not stay still for too long to avoid being taken over by fatigue; you could, for instance, move your spine gently and slowly

- Stare at the stars in the sky while breathing in from the nose deeply and slowly, then breathing out through the mouth

- Pray (mentally)

- Recite a mantra (mentally)

- Hum (quietly, obviously)

- And, **very importantly**, stay inside the shamanic circle!

5.2. Things to avoid

Trying to resist the effects on your mind triggered by ayahuasca can make the experience unbearable. The best advice that I have received (and that I struggled to heed the most) is to relax. My shaman friend once told me: "Everything that ayahuasca wants to show you is destined to teach and guide you." Once again, these are wise words.

You *must* avoid being stricken by fear, panic, or anxiety, no matter what happens.

Very important:

- **Never** disturb a participant during an ayahuasca ceremony unless they have explicitly called for help or are in obvious danger. Unfortunately, I broke this rule during a ceremony, and I still regret it today.

- Do not hesitate to call for help if the experience with ayahuasca becomes too intense. The organizers and shamans are there for that. If there is only one shaman during the ceremony and they are singing, go and see—or call—the organizers and they will either help you or direct you to the right people.

6. After the ceremony

6.1. Each at our own pace

As we saw in the previous two chapters, you should have a period of integration after the ayahuasca ceremony or ceremonies if you want the experience to truly be beneficial. During this process, some participants can experience important changes due to their trauma or physical or mental troubles. Remember that besides the people who partake in ayahuasca ceremonies for spiritual growth, many people do so for health reasons or to treat serious problems, including drug abuse, trauma caused by sexual abuse or physical assault or mental abuse, frantic sexual behavior or nymphomania, alcoholism, excessive aggression, hate, depression, or other negative tendencies and psychological disorders. The time required to cure these disorders depends on the severity of the case and on the individual being treated. If you happen to interact with them, be patient, kind, and compassionate, and **never make any decisions regarding them without consulting** an on-site doctor, the shamans, or the organizers.

6.2. Diet to follow after ayahuasca ceremonies

For your physical and mental well-being, and to ensure the best integration possible of your experiences with ayahuasca, maintain healthy eating habits.

Observe the following diet:

A month following the final ceremony:

Avoid:

- Alcohol

- Red meats, especially pork

- Spicy food, notably chili

The first two weeks following the final ceremony

In addition to the instructions above, avoid:

- Fried food

- Refined sugars

- Ice-cold drinks and ice cream

- Fermented food

- Coffee

- Dairy products

- Citruses (lemon, orange, grapefruit, etc.)

- Raw nuts

7. Before going back to your country

7.1. Importing ayahuasca

You are preparing to leave the country in which you have just taken part in ayahuasca ceremonies or in any other shamanic practices: remember that the customs officials will smile mischievously at your stories about sacred plants, forest spirits, and magical dances that you partook in when they question you about the 'strange' items they have just pulled out from the bottom of your suitcase.

Once again, and at the expense of repeating myself, do not forget that in the eyes of the law, ayahuasca is considered to be a class A drug, like cocaine, heroin, and LSD. The sentences established by the law are very severe and can even go up to the death penalty in some places.

7.2. Importing and exporting shamanic objects

South American countries—among many others—forbid exporting many items. At the airport, it is not uncommon for customs officials to let you check in your luggage, then intercept you and your checked-in luggage for a full search.

Importing shamanic objects is also forbidden in many countries. These items may include feathers, bones, and practically all animal-based items such as drums with animal skin, etc. Inquire before packing your bags.

Good luck, and may you find the answers you are looking for.

With unconditional love.

CEREMONY N° ___   **DATE:** __ / __ / __

List of Decisions

1. _____

2. _____

3. _____

4. _____

5. _____

6. _____

7. _____

8. _____

9. _____

10. _____

11. _____

12. _____

CEREMONY N° ___   DATE: __ / __ / __

Intuitive Development Sheet

1. _____

2. _____

3. _____

4. _____

5. _____

6. _____

7. _____

8. _____

9. _____

10. _____

11. _____

12. _____

CEREMONY N° ___   **DATE: __ / __ / __**

List of Intuitive Answers

1. _____

2. _____

3. _____

4. _____

5. _____

6. _____

7. _____

8. _____

9. _____

10. _____

11. _____

12. _____

CEREMONY N° ___   DATE: __ / __ / __

List of Unique Intuitive Answers

1. _____

2. _____

3. _____

4. _____

5. _____

6. _____

7. _____

8. _____

9. _____

10. _____

11. _____

12. _____

CEREMONY N° ___   **DATE:** __ / __ / __

List of Decisions

1. _____

2. _____

3. _____

4. _____

5. _____

6. _____

7. _____

8. _____

9. _____

10. _____

11. _____

12. _____

CEREMONY N° ___   **DATE: __ / __ / __**

Intuitive Development Sheet

1. _____

2. _____

3. _____

4. _____

5. _____

6. _____

7. _____

8. _____

9. _____

10. _____

11. _____

12. _____

CEREMONY N° ___   **DATE:** __ / __ / __

List of Intuitive Answers

1. _____

2. _____

3. _____

4. _____

5. _____

6. _____

7. _____

8. _____

9. _____

10. _____

11. _____

12. _____

CEREMONY N° ___　　　　　　　　　　　　　　　**DATE:** __ / __ / __

List of Unique Intuitive Answers

1. _____

2. _____

3. _____

4. _____

5. _____

6. _____

7. _____

8. _____

9. _____

10. _____

11. _____

12. _____

![Discovery Publisher logo]

Discovery
Publisher

Discovery Publisher is a multimedia publisher whose mission is to inspire and support personal transformation, spiritual growth and awakening. We strive with every title to preserve the essential wisdom of the author, spiritual teacher, thinker, healer, and visionary artist.

www.ingramcontent.com/pod-product-compliance
Lightning Source LLC
Chambersburg PA
CBHW022121080426

42734CB00006B/205